The
OUTER HEBRIDES HANDBOOK
AND GUIDE

The
Outer Hebrides Handbook
and Guide

KITTIWAKE

Published by **Kittiwake**
3 Glantwymyn Village Workshops,
near Machynlleth, Montgomeryshire SY20 8LY

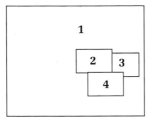

Cover photographs:

1 The Sound of Barra from Pollachar,
South Uist *Dennis Hardley*
2 The brigantine *Jean de la Lune* and
puffer *Eilean Eisdeal* at Lochmaddy, North Uist *David Perrott*
3 Gannets on Boreray *Jim Vaughan*
4 The Flora MacDonald memorial
cairn, South Uist *David Perrott*

Produced for the Rotary Club of Stornoway by Perrott CartoGraphics on
an Apple Macintosh, using Photoshop, Freehand, Streamline and
QuarkXPress. The typeface is Melior

Film output by Litho Link, Welshpool, Montgomeryshire

Printed by MFP Design & Print, Manchester

A catalogue record for this book is available in the British Library

ISBN 0 9511003-5-1

2B/1.0/3.97

INTRODUCTION

On behalf of the community of The Western Isles I have very much pleasure in contributing the preface to this most excellent guidebook for the enthusiastic and committed traveller who wishes to enjoy, in something more than a cursory fashion, the many facets of the life and traditions of our beautiful and peaceful but vibrant archipelago.

The want of an in depth but highly readable and informative guide specific to The Outer Hebrides has been keenly felt for sometime. Much credit is therefore due to the Rotary Club of Stornoway who, under the guidance of Kenneth MacDonald, the Senior Vice President, has brought this nugget of touristic information before the public. Thanks are also due to all the contributors who have given much time and effort to ensuring the publication of this attractive and useful publication.

I know that visitors to our islands will find his or her inevitably enjoyable stay as much enhanced by this book as by the warmth and friendly hospitality of the inhabitants, for truly these are the islands which like to be visited.

A Matheson
Convener Comhairle Nan Eilean

Acknowledgments

This book is a compilation of articles, information
and advice contributed by a considerable number of
willing people throughout the islands who are keen that
any visitor reading this book would be better placed
to understand and appreciate the different culture, scenery
and history before them in The Western Isles.

We would like to thank the following:

Stewart Angus
Comhairle Nan Eilean
Peter Cunningham
Andrew Currie
Alan Frost
Alma Jamieson
Bruce Knight and the staff of the
Meteorological Office, Stornoway & Benbecula
Bill Lawson
Calum MacDonald
Kenneth MacDonald
Colin Scott MacKenzie
Alistair MacLean
Ian MacLeod
Jack MacLeod
John MacLeod
Murdoch MacLeod
Roderick MacLeod
Sandy Matheson
Roderick Morrison
Frank Rennie
Grace Watkins
Edward Young

Editor
David Perrott

CONTENTS

The north of Barra

Background Information

Location and population

The Western Isles consist of a chain of islands about 130 miles long (greater than the distance from London to Cardiff), lying generally north-east to south-west between 30 and 60 miles from the north-west coast of the Scottish mainland. Stretching between latitudes 57–58 N, it shares its northerly position with Gothenburg in southern Sweden, Juneau in Alaska, Uranium City in Saskatchewan and Sverdlosk in Russia.

The ten populated islands are: Lewis, including Great Bernera 20,159; Harris 2,222; Scalpay 382; Berneray 141; North Uist 1,815; Benbecula 1,803; South Uist 2,285; Eriskay 179; Barra 1,316; Vatersay 72, giving a total population for the islands of 29,600.

The major population centre is in and around Stornoway, the only major town within The Western Isles, where 8,132 people live. The remainder of the population is distributed throughout the islands in much smaller units, generally limited to coastal areas and locally collected in typically linear crofting township settlement forms.

The area also encompasses many uninhabited islands such as Scarp, Pabbay, Mingulay and the Monach Isles, plus the outlying islands (also unpopulated) of North Rona, the Flannans, Sula Sgier, St Kilda (a small contingent of soldiers and civilian engineers are based here), the Shiants and Rockall.

Climate (see also page 82)

The average annual rainfall is 1200 mm with about 40% of the rain falling during the months April to September. The annual average of days without rain is about 122, thus rain may be anticipated on two days out of every three. The driest period, averaging about 52 rainless days, is from May to August.

There is more sunshine on the east coast than the west, with an annual average of bright sunshine of 1382 hours, the long term monthly average being: May 210 hours, June 194, July 153, August 152, September 113. A relatively high January sea level temperature is due to the effect on the islands of the North Atlantic Drift – a body of warm Atlantic water originating in the Gulf of Mexico. Although summer temperatures are generally lower than the south of Scotland and England there are much longer hours of summer daylight.

Visitors are advised to bring light but waterproof and windproof outer clothing and sturdy waterproof footwear.

9

Natural environment

The Western Isles is an area of outstanding scientific interest because of its geographical position at the extreme western edge of the European continent and the north western tip of Britain. The area is also the eastern edge of the pasturage of the north Atlantic and is an important boundary between the continental and oceanic influences. The combination of land, sea and inland water have produced landscapes of outstanding, even international significance. These tend to be located on the coast although the hills of North Harris are very important.

There are 40 sites of Special Scientific Interest in the Western Isles having a total area of 38,000 hectares, most being less than 500 hectares but the two largest sites, North Harris and Loch an Duin, North Uist are 12,700 hectares and 15,100 hectares respectively. The majority of these SSSI's have been notified for life science interest, namely botany and zoology.

The machairs support a wide range of plant and animal life and are unique – the juxtaposition of peaty acid soils, loch systems and alkaline machair does not occur to the same extent elsewhere in Britain. Fifteen of the 40 SSSI's are identified as being 'key sites' of national and/or international importance with respect to nature conservation. Four of these sites, all grade 1, have been declared National Nature Reserves.

St. Kilda NNR is of international importance for its oceanic vegetation, breeding sea birds, indigenous fauna of mice, wrens and sheep.

North Rona and Sula Sgier NNR is of international interest for its oceanic vegetation and assemblies of sea birds and grey seals.

Monach Isles NNR is of national importance for its coastal habitats of calcareous dunes and machair which are rich in flowers and provide an undisturbed pasture for barnacle geese in winter and a nursery for grey seals.

Loch Druidibeg NNR is of international importance for its open fresh water system which has a wide range of trophic levels with related communities of plants and animals, it is also of national importance for its coastal habitats of lagoon, dune and machair.

Balranald Bay and Loch nan Feithean SSSI include an RSPB reserve of national importance.

Scottish Natural Heritage has identified three main areas in The Western Isles as being of outstanding scenic value:

South Lewis, Harris and North Uist 109,600 ha.
St. Kilda 900 ha.
South Uist Machair 6,100 ha.
This area in total 116,000 ha. is 40% of the total land area of The Western Isles.

Built environment

The Western Isles contain many archeological and historic sites of appeal both to the specialist and to the general tourist. Prehistoric forts, wheel houses, chambered cairns and monoliths are among the archeological remains; fortified keeps, churches and ecclesiastical ruins are among the historic attractions. In the list of Ancient Monuments in Scotland there are 40 entries for prehistoric monuments in The Western Isles together with three listings under 'Crosses and Carved Stones', twelve listings under 'Ecclesiastical' and four under 'Secular' monuments. Five of these monuments are of national importance and are in the guardianship of the Secretary of State for Scotland. These are:

Stein a Cleit Chambered Cairn and Stone Circle at Shader

Lewis Black House, Arnol

Doune Carloway Broch

Callanish Standing Stones – *all in Lewis*, and:

St Clements Church Rodel *in Harris*

Sadly, interpretive facilities in general associated with most of these sites and monuments have been confined to voluntary efforts together with a certain amount of informative signposting by the Ancient Monuments Inspectorate of the Scottish Development Department.

With the exception of Stornoway the built environment throughout The Western Isles is characteristic of crofting communities. That is linear with detached houses on individual plots of land. In the past virtually all domestic buildings had thatched roofs and once unoccupied these buildings deteriorated rapidly as a result of the type of construction employed and the effect of climatic conditions. The dearth of building materials, especially timber, caused materials from abandoned or redundant buildings to be re-used and consequently there are relatively few pre-1900 buildings in The Western Isles, especially outwith Stornoway. In Stornoway there are some surviving commercial, ecclesiastical and domestic buildings dating back to the 18thC.

There are 149 listed buildings of special architectural or historic interest in The Western Isles. Of these 12 are of national or more than local interest and 25 are 'group listings', most of which are groups of traditional thatched dwellings. Sadly many of these buildings are in poor condition. There are two conservation areas, one a group of thatched cottages at Garenin (worth a visit to catch the flavour of a seaside crofting hamlet) and the other the town centre area of Stornoway, which provides an interesting and stimulating walkabout lasting one hour. There is a detailed leaflet on this entitled *Stornoway* by Mary Bone.

THE HISTORY OF LEWIS

Mystery surrounds the origin of the first inhabitants of The Outer Hebrides but it is thought that they were a Mediterranean people, megalithic builders of the late Stone Age or early Bronze Age, who colonised the west of Britain by sea and built Stonehenge and the Callanish Stones in the second millennium BC. They were probably followed by migrating Celts from central Europe about 500 BC, amongst whom were a curious race who settled in the Highlands and Islands of Scotland only, where they built brochs, unique to that area, and of which there is a fine example at Carloway. The Scandinavian influence became predominant in The Western Isles following the Battle of Hafursfiord in 885 when Harald Hargager gained absolute control of Norway, with the result that the dissident lesser Kings had to take to their long boats and find other worlds to conquer – such as the Hebrides, Shetland and Orkney, Ireland, Iceland and the Isle of Man.

The original clans on Lewis are said to have been the Morrisons, Nicolsons and MacAulays – all of whom are thought to have had Norse backgrounds. The Macleods, however, dominated much of the history of Lewis, and are reputed to have been the descendants of Harald the Black of Iceland.

In 1598 James VI entered into a contract with some 'Gentlemen Adventurers' from Fife 'To plant policy and civilisation in the hitherto most barbarous Isle of Lewis, with Rona-Lews and Trotternish, and to develop the extraordinarily rich resources of the same for the public good and the King's profit'. The syndicate of Adventurers were to be free from any payment of feu duty until 1600 because of their initial expenses, and the contract goes on to lay down regulations for the government of the Burghs of Barony which the syndicate were empowered to elect, and of any ports and havens they might create. Provision was made in the contract for the building of four Parish Churches on Lewis and Rona, and it was ordained that a process of forfeiture be prepared against the Chiefs and a new title made out in favour of the Adventurers. The last clause of the document stipulated that no part of the Highlands or Isles should be disposed of or feued but to Lowland men and the Adventurers were to teach Lewis men religion and humanity by deporting them or exterminating them. They sailed for Stornoway in 1598 accompanied by a number of miscellaneous tradesmen. At the time of the invasion of Lewis the island was in the hands of Murdoch and Neil Macleod (illegitimate sons of the Macleod chief), who stubbornly resisted the invaders but their resistance finally broke down and Stornoway

The broch at Carloway

Castle fell. The colonists built their town of stone, timber and turf. South Beach, Stornoway, now covers the site. Neil Macleod, who had come to an agreement with the colonists, fell out with them and he, with his brother Tormod, stormed the colonists' fort and drove them out. King James VI was rather annoyed as he had hoped to earn some money from the venture. He forced the Adventurers to set up a second expedition but, because of the Union of the Crowns in 1603, the second expedition did not take place until 1605.

Neil harried the Adventurers during the winter 1605 without achieving any success but in 1607 he destroyed their camp, having entered it by trickery. The Lowlanders were ruined and returned home but in that year, 1607, a third attempt was made to plant a colony on Lewis and a Charter was granted to James, Master of Balmerino; Sir James Spens of Wormiston; and Sir George Hay of Netherliff. It is from this Charter that the town of Stornoway got its status as a Burgh of Barony.

Lord Kintail, the able chief of the Clan MacKenzie, had purchased the right to Lewis from the Fife Adventurers, but he died in 1611 and was succeeded by his fourteen year old son, whose guardian was Ruaridh Mackenzie, his uncle and the tutor of Kintail. The tutor of Kintail had a claim to Lewis having married the daughter of Torquil Conanach, a putative but repudiated son of the old chief of the Macleods, and he now applied himself to the task of chasing Neil Macleod and his followers out of their stronghold on Berisay, an island in Loch Roag. Legend says that he gave orders to seize the wives, children and other relatives of Neil Macleod and his friends on Berisay. He then had them placed at low tide on a rock sufficiently near the island for the occupants to hear and see them. He told Neil that, unless he and his companions surrendered immediately, their helpless relatives would be left to drown on the return of the tide. Neil and his followers capitulated on condition that they were allowed to leave Lewis and Neil took refuge with his kinsman Ruaridh Macleod of Harris. Ruaridh Macleod however handed over Neil and his son Donald to the Council in Edinburgh, for which he received the honour of a knighthood. Neil Macleod was tried in Edinburgh in March 1613 on serious charges to which he pleaded guilty, having been examined through an interpreter. Neil Macleod's sons and other descendants of the Macleod Chiefs gave a considerable amount of trouble in the Hebrides and elsewhere for a number of years, but gradually they disappeared from the scene and so Lewis became the undisputed possession of the Mackenzies.

In 1623 Lord Kintail was created Earl of Seaforth and, in 1628, went to London with the object of securing from the King a patent for the elevation of Stornoway into a Royal Burgh. He obtained a charter from the King but the Convention of Royal Burghs of Scotland refused to give effect to it after 'mature deliberation', as the charter would be prejudicial to the Royal Burghs of Tain and Inverness. The Privy Council, to whom appeal was made, did nothing and Seaforth failed, with the charter being cancelled in 1630.

The King took a great interest in the Lewis fisheries, from which it was estimated there would be a substantial profit each year. Some English settlers came to Stornoway for the purposes of prosecuting the fishing industry but were successfully opposed by mainland and Dutch fishermen.

Charles I gave a charter for Lewis to Seaforth in 1637 and, in 1678, when the Seaforth estates were transferred to three members of the Mackenzie Clan, Stornoway was reserved for the Crown but without Royal Burgh status.

Because of an incident in 1653 Cromwell ordered an expedition to Lewis to punish the then Earl of Seaforth. They established themselves on Goat Island in Stornoway Harbour and in the area between South Beach Street and James Street. Stornoway Castle was dismantled by the English garrison at this time. A plaque on the Maritime Buildings commemorates its existence and the remains can be seen under the ferry pier.

After the Battle of Culloden in 1746 Prince Charles Edward Stuart arrived in Benbecula, whence he travelled to Arnish on the far side of Stornoway harbour. He hoped to charter a vessel at Stornoway that would take him to France and sent Donald Macleod, a guide and navigator, into the town to endeavour to obtain a vessel ostensibly bound for Orkney but really, of course, to take the Prince to France. Donald Macleod went to work very cautiously and ultimately found a suitable ship, a brig of 40 tons owned and commanded by a Captain MacAulay. He appears, however, to have given away the object of

Lews Castle, Stornoway

chartering a boat to Captain MacAulay, who then indicated the following day that he wished to withdraw from the bargain. Prince
Charles, who had sailed up Loch Seaforth, made the rest of the journey on foot until they reached the moor at Arnish, where Donald
Macleod took him provisions at the house of a Mrs Mackenzie of
Kildun. When Donald Macleod went back to Stornoway to resume
negotiations for a ship he found the town in an uproar – apparently
the news had spread that the Prince intended to come to Stornoway.
Donald Macleod then admitted to a number of self appointed officers, who were engaged in holding a council of war, that the Prince
was on Lewis but not with the five hundred men rumoured, but only
two attendants. The people of the town did not want to get themselves involved in confrontation with the Government although sym-
pathetic to the Prince, and they therefore indicated to Donald
Macleod that they had not the slightest desire to harm the Prince nor
to meddle with him in any way. Though they would not betray him,
despite the incredible award of £30,000 on his head, they would not
permit him to enter the town, nor would they give him a ship, nor

would they provide him with a pilot to take him to Poolewe where there was some chance of his finding a vessel. Donald Macleod returned to Arnish and told the Prince what had happened. It was obviously unsafe for them to remain and preparations were thereafter made for departure. They slept that night on the moor close to the loch at Arnish, which is now known as Prince Charlie's Loch. A commemorative cairn was later erected above the loch. Eventually they made their way via Lochmaddy to Benbecula and South Uist, whence with Flora MacDonald, a stepdaughter of Captain Hugh MacDonald of Armadale, they sailed over the Minch to Skye accompanied by the Prince, dressed in female clothing and passing himself off as Betty Burke, Flora's maid.

In 1844 Mr James Matheson of the Jardine Matheson Company of Hong Kong bought Lewis for £190,000 from the last of the Mackenzies. Mr Matheson, who later became Sir James Matheson, transformed the face of Lewis. He built Lews Castle on the site of Seaforth Lodge, which had been built by the Mackenzies and began afforestation of the area bounded by the Lochs Road, the River Creed and Stornoway Harbour, moving citizens who had lived in that area into alternative accommodation in Stornoway. New houses were built in Stornoway, gas and water work companies were established and harbour facilities were so improved that by 1849 the townsfolk of Stornoway were reaping the benefit of all these undertakings.

However, the failure of the potato crop in 1845 led to famine between 1845 and 1850. Mr Matheson, as he then was, endeavoured to assist his tenants by providing work in road making and repairing, building quays, erecting dykes to protect the cultivated land from animals, draining suitable moorland to create arable land and generally trying to relieve their distress.

Sir James, who received his Baronetcy in 1850, established a very profitable patent slip in Stornoway Harbour, provided a regular shipping service to the mainland, and constructed around 150 miles of roads. He built a number of sporting lodges, including those at Grimersta, Morsgail and Uig.

In 1918 Lord Leverhulme, founder of Lever Brothers, bought the estate from the Matheson family. Lord Leverhulme's plans were for the development of a major fishing industry with ancillary industries such as weaving, land reclamation, afforestation etc, together with the building of roads and a railway system. He planned to develop the harbour facilities to accommodate his plans for the expansion of the fishing industry. He wanted to establish a chain of companies under his own control and to have the fishing industry in his hands from the time the fish left the sea until it arrived on the table. Stornoway was to become the chief town of the West Highlands or the 'Venice of the North' as he called it, with an increase of population from four thousand to nine thousand. He planned the Lewis Light Railway system which was to have three spurs from

Stornoway, one going through Balallan to Aline, the second to Callanish and Carloway and then round to Barvas to join on the line from Barvas to Stornoway, but allowing for a spur going from Barvas to Ness. Lord Leverhulme was extremely generous. He established a gas supply, laundry and dairy for the town of Stornoway and also planned electricity for the streets. There was, however, considerable demand for land by returning ex-servicemen, who knew that land settlement was taking place in other parts of the Highlands and Islands and could see no reason why the same was not happening on Lewis. The spending by Lord Leverhulme of about £200,000 a year in the island was not, in the eyes of these men, acceptable if the choice was between that and the possession of a croft. Land raids began in March 1919 on the farms of Tong, Coll and Gress, and were followed by raids in other parishes.

Lord Leverhulme stopped all his island operations in May 1920, following which the Secretary of State for Scotland was urged to persuade Lord Leverhulme to continue with his schemes. The Secretary of State for Scotland reminded Lord Leverhulme in August 1920 that, unless he was prepared to resume his schemes, there would no longer be any justification for the Government to refrain from exercising the statutory powers possessed by the Board of Agriculture to meet the demand for land holdings – powers which had been held in abeyance in order that Lord Leverhulme be given the opportunity if he wished to proceed with his own schemes. Lord Leverhulme insisted that before he resumed his work on Lewis, the Government should give an assurance that there would be no raiding for the next ten years and that the raiders would vacate the farms. In October 1920 the Lord Advocate visited the raiders at Back and Coll to discuss the matter with them. Following this they left the farms in anticipation that they would be allowed to return in the spring but, in the meantime, support was mounting for Lord Leverhulme as a result of which Mr Munro, the Secretary of State, advised Lord Leverhulme that he believed it was in the best interests of the community as a whole that the assurance sought by Lord Leverhulme must be given. Lord Leverhulme then indicated that he was prepared to resume operations by the end of March or early April.

Lord Leverhulme, however, was in financial difficulties by January 1921 with the result that, when the work was resumed in April on a much reduced scale there was considerable unease. The Coll and Gress raiders promptly raided the farms again and Lord Leverhulme was reminded by the Secretary of State that the pledge of non-intervention by the Government had been granted on condition that his schemes were in operation and, as this was not not the case, there was no reason why land settlement should not be undertaken. The attitude of the Secretary of State caused Lord Leverhulme much annoyance. There was considerable distress by the end of 1921 owing to the cessation of Lord Leverhulme's projects and relief work had to be started. The Lewis District Committee were given a grant of £38,000 in 1922 by the Board of Agriculture, of which £10,000 was to be spent on the breaking of road metal and the re-surfacing of existing roads, with the balance being used for making new roads. This was a great shock for the economy of the island as, quite obviously, a grant of £38,000 did not compare with the £200,000 Lord Leverhulme had been spending each year. This was the end of Lord Leverhulme's plans for Lewis and, in disgust, he concentrated his efforts on Harris, for which he had already made plans, where they were generally welcomed.

He finally decided to offer the island of Lewis to the people and proposed the formation of a Stornoway Trust to administer the Parish of Stornoway, with the freehold of all crofts (with the exception of those occupied by the ex-raiders) to be offered as a gift to their present occupiers. The rest of the island was to be given to the Lewis District Committee and the crofts there offered to the crofters on the same basis as those in the Parish of Stornoway. The Stornoway Town Council accepted his offer and presumably acted on behalf of the Parish of Stornoway although they really did not have any jurisdiction outwith the boundaries of the Burgh of Stornoway. The Lewis District Committee refused the offer as did the majority of the crofters, with only 41 of them accepting his gift. The Stornoway Trust was then established covering the area of the Parish of Stornoway, and becoming unique in land ownership, with the ratepayers within the Parish electing their own landlords. This they still do. The remaining parts of the island were sold to individuals or syndicates. Lord Leverhulme had failed.

The Leverhulme era had two clear effects on the economy of the island of Lewis. Firstly the establishment of the Stornoway Trust, which is a model of land ownership by the people living in the area, and secondly the mass emigrations which took place following the failure of Leverhulme's schemes. In April 1923 the Canadian Pacific vessel *Metagama* sailed to Canada with 300 emigrants and one year later the *Marloch* took away 290 emigrants, followed a few weeks later by the *Canada* with 270 more, making a total of 860 emigrants, mostly youngsters who had never been out of the island before. Some of these emigrants to Canada were successful in making new lives for themselves but a great number of them met with difficulties and hardships, and over the years those that were able returned back to Lewis.

A greater tragedy had afflicted Lewis some years earlier when, on the 1st January 1919, H M Yacht *Iolaire*, returning with ex-servicemen to Lewis, foundered on the reef outside Stornoway Harbour known as the 'Beasts of Holm'. 205 of the people aboard lost their lives with only 79 people being saved. Most of these survivors owe their lives to the strength and courage of John F Macleod from Port of Ness who jumped from the boat with a heaving line and with great

Achmore, Lewis

difficulty swam ashore. Wedging himself amongst the boulders on the beach he hauled a hawser ashore, along which most of the survivors struggled.

It is not difficult to imagine the disastrous effect on the island of the *Iolaire* disaster and the mass emigrations following the Leverhulme era because, in the main, the people who lost their lives were the young, energetic, potential leaders of the island community.

The main sources of employment between the two World Wars were fishing, Harris Tweed and, mainly as a subsidiary, crofting. It is interesting to note that Lewis, which had a population of over 28,000 in 1921, dropped to over 21,000 in the census of 1931. Like every other community in the United Kingdom, Lewis men and women served in the Second World War and the island saw the presence of military personnel with barracks in various places, including the lawns of Lews Castle, which was then a naval hospital. The Royal Air Force had a presence at the aerodrome built on the old Stornoway golf course.

Following the war came the process of rebuilding, with a great deal of effort being carried out by Stornoway Town Council. Large portions of the old town of Stornoway were demolished and improvements implemented. House building for returning ex-servicemen and others was carried out at an accelerated rate. In 1952 Lewis obtained its first and only college when the Stornoway Trust handed over Lews Castle, which had been built by Sir James Matheson, to the Education Authority of Ross and Cromarty which converted it for use as a Technical College. In the 1970s there was established within Stornoway Harbour at Glumaig Bay (Arnish) an off-shore oil fabrication yard which has made a significant contribution to employment in the islands since that date.

The main change, which took place in 1974, was the establishment of The Western Isles as a single, multipurpose unit of local government. Prior to the Local Government (Scotland) Act 1973 there were three tiers of local government in the Western Isles with Harris and the Uists and Barra being part of Inverness County Council and Lewis being part of Ross and Cromarty County Council. The second tier of local government was the Town Council of the Burgh of Stornoway and the third District Councils for the various islands. There is little doubt that the establishment of Comhairle nan Eilean (Western Isles Island Council) has been of great benefit to the islands.

THE HISTORY OF HARRIS

The early history of Harris is almost certainly identical to that of Lewis, with the inhabitants being probably Dalriadic Scots or Picts followed by the Scandinavians and then by the Scots Irish or Celts. W. C. MacKenzie in his *History of the Outer Hebrides* states that the name 'Harris' is unquestionably of Scandinavian origin and that it means a province or territory ruled by a *hersir* who was not only the hereditary head of the community but its prophet, priest and king.

Harris, which was given to Tormod son of Leod (progenitor of the Clan MacLeod), at the same time as Lewis was given to his brother Torquil, remained in the possession of the MacLeods, who were subservient to the Lord of the Isles, for five hundred years. This was considerably longer than Lewis remained in the possession of *Siol Torquil*. The earliest Charter given to the MacLeods of Harris was given by David II in 1343, and this charter also gave them two thirds of Glenelg. It is difficult to trace the names of the earlier Chiefs of MacLeod of Harris, except that the original Tormod MacLeod was succeeded by his son Malcolm and that thereafter there was a John MacLeod who had a son William Dubh MacLeod, whose son was Alistair Crotach MacLeod. This Alistair Crotach MacLeod received a Charter from James IV in 1498 and was a trusted friend of the king. A sister of his was the second wife of Gilleonan of Barra.

The history of Harris does not appear to be as bloody as that of Lewis, where many battles were fought over the chieftainship and ownership of the island. There is however one incident of some significance when Donald Gorm MacDonald, who had, in 1596, obtained a Charter of Sleat and North Uist with lands in South Uist and Benbecula, and had married a sister of Ruari MacLeod of Harris, took a violent dislike to his wife and packed her off to her friends, repudiating her as his wife. This roused the ire of Rory Mor of Harris who asked Donald Gorm to take his wife back. Donald Gorm not only refused, but divorced her and married a sister of MacKenzie of Kintail, whereupon Rory Mor MacLeod took his revenge by devastating Trotternish and Donald Gorm retaliated by invading Harris which he wasted, killing some of the inhabitants and carrying away much booty. Rory MacLeod then instructed his cousin, Donald Glas, to invade North Uist and carry off from Teampull na Trionaid (Trinity Church) at Carinish the goods which the Uist people had placed there for safety. Donald Glas proceeded to obey these instructions with a force of 40 men but was met by John MacIan MacDonald, a near relative of Donald Gorm, with 12 men who completely routed the MacLeods although they themselves were outnumbered. Rory Mor MacLeod was so disheartened that he retired to Rodel, Harris. One of the participants on the MacDonald side in the affray was driven by a storm to take refuge at Rodel while on his way to report to Donald Gorm. He and his followers were hospitably entertained by Rory Mor, who was initially unaware of the identity of his guests. When it became known it strained the strict laws of Highland hospitality almost to breaking point. Some of the MacLeods, however, set fire to the MacDonalds' dormitory during the night but the birds had wisely flown, not wishing to put too great a strain on their hosts' generosity! The final battle in this feud was fought on the shoulder of one of the Cuillin hills in Skye, with the MacLeods again being defeated, but the Privy Council intervened in the quarrel and eventually settled the matter.

The MacLeods of Harris were involved in many of the political manoeuvrings of the day and, indeed, in many of the battles, but none of these affected their tenure of Harris under the Lordship of the Isles, until the Lordship of the Isles passed to the Crown. In 1745, at the time of the Rising led by Bonnie Prince Charlie, the Chief of the MacLeods of Harris was Norman MacLeod, who had ruined himself by gambling and wastage of his resources – following which he raised the rents of his tenants. This obviously placed a great burden on the impoverished people of Harris, and the influence of the general emigrations spreading throughout the Highlands at that time was felt. Indeed if it were not for the influence of the Chief's grandson and successor in 1772 there would have been a mass emigration from the estates. This grandson succeeded his grandfather in the year 1772 and inherited the property and the debt, which amounted at that time to £50,000. He was General Norman MacLeod, a very distinguished soldier, and when he was abroad his Commissioners, in 1779, sold Harris and St Kilda to Captain Alexander MacLeod for the sum of £15,000.

Captain MacLeod appears to have had an enlightened policy in his relations with his tenants. He encouraged the fishing industry and effected improvements in the harbour accommodation. He built a storehouse for salt, casks, meal, etc, and established a factory for spinning woollen and cotton thread and twine for herring nets. He brought over some east coast fishermen with Orkney Yawls to teach the people, and erected a boathouse capable of containing nine boats with their tackle. His interest in the fishing industry led him to advance money for boats, furnish the fishermen with the necessities at cost price, provide them with cottages and potato ground rent free, and to pay the full market value for their fish. Captain MacLeod also restored the Church of St Clements at Rodel, built a schoolhouse and an inn, constructed roads from his two quays to the village and from there to the west side of the island. He introduced improved mills.

His grandson sold Harris in 1834 to the Earl of Dunmore, who in

The Church of St Clements at Rodel

turn sold North Harris to the Scotts in 1868. This estate included the islands of Scalpay and Scarp, and Tarbert. South Harris, including the islands of Taransay, Bernera and some of the other islands remained in the ownership of Viscount Fincastle, who was the only son of the Earl of Dunmore. The islands of Ensay and Pabbay in the Sound of Harris passed into the ownership of a Captain William Stewart.

The Earl of Dunmore had some considerable impact, as it is said that his mother, the Dowager Countess of Dunmore, bought a length of tweed in 1842 and subsequently, because of her promotion of the cloth among her friends, the Harris Tweed industry was born (see Harris Tweed, page 45).

There is an assumption that Lord Leverhulme, who had purchased Lewis in 1918, concentrated his energies on Harris, only after having failed in his schemes for the development of Lewis, but this is not the case. Lord Leverhulme was anxious to develop both islands at the same time. He did hope to bring his trawlers into Carloway and Obbe but subsequent recession deprived him of the former and he had to transfer his hopes to Obbe.

Lord Leverhulme was welcomed in Harris, where he indicated that he wished to develop the small village of Obbe and create a large fishing harbour there. He indicated at a public meeting that his proposals were dependent upon the people of Harris accepting five conditions:

– That they would work full-heartedly with him in a spirit of co-operation

– That, if certain crofts had to be cleared for the development of his schemes at Obbe, the crofters would accept alternative crofts elsewhere

– That the same principle would apply if certain common grazings had to be developed

– That there would be no farm raids

– That any unforeseen difficulties that might arise would be dealt with in the same spirit of co-operation as would have to prevail for all the other four conditions.

These conditions were acceptable to the people involved who by and large kept the promises implicit in them, although there were two instances where there was a breach. One being when six crofters from the Bays district raided the farm at Rodel in April 1921, as a consequence of which they were prosecuted and received forty days imprisonment, which they served in full. These crofters did not have the support of the community on Harris. The second incident occurred in December 1922 when three men from the north of South Harris pegged out claims for themselves on the Rodel farm, but left when a strong force of one hundred and fifty men challenged them, with the assurance that they would get work. This assurance was fulfiled.

There is some doubt as to how the name of Obbe was changed to Leverburgh. Lord Leverhulme himself claimed that the people of the area had asked that it be done in recognition of the work that was being carried out there.

Lord Leverhulme wanted to develop the fishing of the west coast of Harris with boats fishing the Atlantic coast, and to also develop handloom weaving. In order to achieve this at Leverburgh he proposed to build three quays where fifty herring drifters could lie alongside, and an inner harbour for up to two hundred boats. He also set out to construct initially temporary accommodation for his workers, packing sheds and a kipper house. The harbour work started in 1920, and by the time of Leverhulme's death in 1925 there had been considerable work completed in Leverburgh. Six houses had been completed, eight were half completed and work on another eight had been commenced.

Because of Leverhulme's financial constraints, the workforce at Leverburgh was reduced from 260 to 120 in 1921 and the other works on Harris were temporarily closed.

There is some doubt as to whether Obbe was an appropriate site for the harbour planned by Leverhulme because of navigational difficulties. Indeed he was advised that the development of harbour facilities in west Loch Tarbert and east Loch Tarbert would give the fish-

Urgha, near Tarbert, Harris

ing fleet the flexibility of operating off both the east and west coast of the island.

Lord Leverhulme purchased Bunavoneader in 1922, where there had previously been a whaling station operated by a Norwegian company. This scheme of Leverhulme's failed although he had purchased three Norwegian vessels to catch whales. Unfortunately there was no market for the whale oil and whale meat. One of his schemes for the development of the tweed industry involved the construction of a spinning mill at Geocrab but this scheme also failed. There was a slump in the tweed industry at the time, and the Harris weavers perceived the destruction of handloom weaving by virtue of the greater industrialisation of the industry, as evidenced by its development in Stornoway and Lewis.

The fishing at Leverburgh began well in the spring of 1924, but by late summer and autumn the figures were considerably reduced. Leverhulme himself left for the last time in 1924, although it was not intended that it should be his last visit. He had, despite his cut-backs in expenditure on his schemes, negotiated with the Secretary of State for the construction of four roads on Harris. Work commenced on them in 1924 on condition that he himself would pay half of the cost. These roads were on the Tarbert to Kyles Scalpay road; the Amhuinnsuidhe Castle to Hushinish road; the Leverburgh to Finsbay road; and the Bays Road from Grosebay to Finsbay. While he was resident on Harris, Leverhulme stayed in Borve Lodge, which had remained in the possession of the Earl of Dunmore until 1923. He died in 1925 following a visit to the Congo, and all his schemes on Harris were immediately abandoned by his successors, with the estates and developments being sold for considerably less than the expenditure on them.

Since the Leverhulme era on Harris there has really been no main source of employment although, for a time, the mill at Geocrab, taken over by one of the Stornoway Tweed concerns, ran with varying success. Scalpay has had considerable fishing employment on the catching side for a number of years, and they have been very successful. This island also had a shipping company which owned several vessels carrying small cargoes round the west coast of Scotland. There is still some crofting supplemented by whatever employment can be obtained in areas such as road-works, crafts and the tourist industry. Because of its scenic beauty, with the hills of North Harris and some of the most beautiful beaches in the world on the south west of the island, it is particularly suitable for tourist development.

THE HISTORY OF THE UISTS AND BENBECULA

The earliest identifiable date of habitation of these islands is the period of Norse occupation from the 9thC to 13thC, although there is a mass of evidence of much earlier occupation, of an indefinite period, indicated by the earth houses, wheel houses and the defensive island duns found in many lochs. These duns vary from amorphous heaps of stones to highly organised broch structures, such as Dun Torcuil in North Uist. The island duns generally have a dog-legged underwater causeway to facilitate friendly access. In addition to the various types of living accommodation there are, throughout the islands, numerous barps, where the more pretentious natives found their last resting places. These consist of vast cairns of stone enclosing a central chamber, and there are fine examples at Langas in North Uist and at Frebost in South Uist. Among the interesting domestic sites, Udal in North Uist, which is still the site of archeological excavation, shows continuous occupation from the pre-Viking period right through to medieval times.

The clan that has dominated the history of the Uists and Benbecula is the Macdonalds. When Lewis passed into the control of the Earldom of Ross the Uists and Benbecula were passed into the hands of Allan MacRuari, who also received the Island of Barra in 1309 as a reward from Robert the Bruce for the MacRuari's patriotic service.

His daughter Aimie succeeded to the Uists estates and married John MacDonald, Lord of the Isles. He changed sides between the English and the Scots whenever he could gain maximum benefit for himself. He later divorced Aimie upon securing a papal dispensation. She then, being a very pious woman, devoted herself to the rebuilding of Trinity Church in North Uist, the building of an Oratory in Grimsay, and a castle at Borve in Benbecula.

The Uists were now in the hands of the MacDonalds, Lords of the Isles, and were to pass through several generations to John (a grandson of Aimie) Lord of the Isles and also Earl of Ross. As a result of him entering into independent treaties with Edward IV of England in 1462, King James III of Scotland declared him a traitor and forfeited his estates. These estates were later offered by the king for lease, but John's grandson Donald Dubh, who claimed the heirship to the Lord of the Isles, escaped custody and fled to his Uncle Torquil Macleod of Lewis who sounded the call to arms for the islanders. In 1503 under the youthful Donald Dubh, they spread over Lochaber, Bute and Arran, devastating the whole country in their line of march. Finally, after the failed insurrection of Donald Dubh and his imprisonment initially in Edinburgh Castle and then in Stirling Castle. The Earl of Argyll was made King's Lieutenant of the Uists and Barra.

The men of Uist were also involved in the Jacobite Rising of 1715 when, at the battle of Sheriffmuir, they fought on the right wing of the first line of the Jacobite Army under Sir Donald Macdonald and Allan Macdonald of Clanranald. The Highlanders on this wing had a memorable charge which scattered the government troops like chaff, but the ultimate result was a drawn battle, where Allan Macdonald of Clanranald lost his life. Sir Donald Macdonald, having held out for some time in Skye, fled to North Uist for safety. French ships arrived at that stage with supplies for the Jacobite army, but returned to France with about a hundred Jacobite officers on board.

Prince Charles Edward Stewart set out in 1745 from France to rally the clans to arms. He landed in Eriskay first before heading to Moidart on the mainland. It was after the final failure of the uprising at Culloden in 1745 that the Prince made his escape via the Uists. He landed in Benbecula, then made his way towards Stornoway in the hope of finding a vessel to help him escape. When no one was prepared to help he returned to Benbecula. He spent weeks travelling from various hiding places (huts and caves all down the east coast of Benbecula and South Uist) until, when hiding on an island off Loch Boisdale, Captain Hugh Macdonald of Armadale in Skye sent a secret message to him advising him to try and reach Lady Margaret MacDonald of Skye who would help him return to France.

Captain MacDonald of Skye, in spite of being in charge of a company of militia and serving the government, was still a Jacobite at heart. He proposed that his stepdaughter Flora MacDonald, who was visiting her brother near Ormacleit, should return to Skye with the Prince dressed in female clothing as her maid Betty Burke. Avoiding all the troops and ships guarding the coastline they managed to make their escape from Benbecula to Skye.

There were two innovations in the 18thC which had a profound effect on the history of the islands. At that time the potato was first introduced. The fact that it could be harvested regardless of the vagaries of the weather soon established it as an abundant food source, with the consequence that an increase in the population followed.

About the same time the manufacture of kelp (an alkaline ash used in the making of glass, soap and linen) by the burning of seaweed was introduced. In place of the previous method of paying rent in the form of agricultural produce, tenants were now required to pay by engaging in this labour intensive industry. They were encouraged to move to the coasts to be nearer to their raw material and as a result they were less able to cultivate the land, allowing the introduction of commercial farmers, who could pay an additional *money* rent to the proprietors.

The successive failure of the kelp industry after the end of the

The remains of Trinity Church, North Uist

Napoleonic War and the failure of the potato crop in 1846 and 1847, led to massive forced emigration. Six hundred people emigrated from North Uist to North America in 1828. Twenty years later a further five hundred emigrated.

In South Uist the new proprietor, Colonel Gordon of Cluny, induced people to assemble at Loch Boisdale by deceitful means, then forced them to board vessels which transported them to Upper Canada, where they were left to starve. The population of Benbecula and South Uist dropped by 2000 between 1841 and 1861 as a result of famine and the proprietor's policy of wholesale expatriation.

The evacuation led to no increase in the land available to those who remained, since sheep farmers moved in. The congested peripheral lands and off-shore islands forced the inhabitants to look to supplement their subsistence agriculture by fishing.

Although more crofting land became available upon the breaking up of large farms early in this century, agriculture has changed to a pastoral rather than an arable type and is, in the main, a part-time occupation supplementing employment in the service industries. In some of the west coast machair areas there are still a few self-sufficient farms.

Periodically seaweed has been exploited as a raw material for its iodine content and more recently, for its alginate, although on each occasion it has been supplanted by cheaper foreign imports.

A most important feature of the Uists is still their cultural impact. There is an impressive native courtesy (without servility) which is also manifest by the warm hospitality frequently proffered by those less able to afford it. There is a wealth of traditionally acquired oral poetry and prose in Gaelic, including ballads, work songs, heroic and historical tales, some of which have remained virtually unchanged in folk memory for a thousand years.

THE HISTORY OF BARRA

The premier Barra clan are The MacNeils, who are of very ancient lineage indeed. They originated from Ireland and were in possession of Barra prior to the Norse invasion, perhaps as early as the 9thC. Their stronghold of Kisimul Castle was built some time around the 13thC. Their chiefs are distinguished as being acknowledged as Chiefs of the Clan MacNeil in Scotland. Their local importance is illustrated by the custom of a herald sounding a horn from the battlements of Kisimul Castle and proclaiming aloud in Gaelic: 'Here ye people, and listen, oh ye nations! The great MacNeil of Barra having finished his meal the Princes of the earth may dine!'. Gilleonan MacNeil received from Alexander, Lord of the Isles, a Charter of Barra and Boisdale in South Uist in 1427, which was confirmed by the Crown in 1495.

At the end of the 16thC Ruari MacNeil was a noted pirate, raiding Dutch or French vessels. He did, however, decide to pursue his piracy off the coast of Ireland with the result that his exploits came to the attention of Queen Elizabeth of England who complained of MacNeil's activities to King James VI. James designated Roderick MacKenzie, who was afterwards to become the Tutor of Kintail, to seize MacNeil. He disguised himself as a peaceful skipper and arrived at Kisimul Castle on a merchantman, with the greater number of his men under hatches and the remainder posing as the crew. Ruari MacNeil was invited aboard to sample the brandy and wines and, after some drinking had taken place, the men under the hatches rushed out and made the whole party prisoners. The vessel then weighed anchor and left. MacNeil was allowed to keep the estate of Barra but MacKenzie became the feudal superior of the estate.

The Captain of Clan Ranald attacked MacNeil in North Boisdale (which was part of the Barra property) in 1601 and drove him out of Uist forcing him to take refuge on one of the remote islets of Barra, with Boisdale passing into the possession of Clanranald.

The MacNeils of Barra were not the only ones who augmented their incomes by piracy. A ship from Leith with a cargo of tea, wines and general merchandise was, in 1625, rounding Barra Head bound northwards, when Clanranald and some of his men boarded and plundered her. There was a similar exploit on the part of Clanranald in 1636 when an English barque, named the *Susannah*, was driven ashore on Barra. The men of Barra arranged with the Captain for salvage and towed the ship into the harbour but, on landing, were confronted by Clanranald with three hundred of his men who then seized the vessel.

In 1794 two hundred natives of Barra were induced by false

Kisimul Castle, Castlebay

promises to emigrate to Prince Edward Island. When they arrived there was nothing for them and they would surely have died of starvation had they not been helped by the earlier colonists. When the news of this venture came back to Barra, those who had sold their effects in order to leave for America decided to remain at home.

In 1838 General MacNeil, the then owner, went bankrupt, because of the failure of the chemical works he had erected at Northbay for the manufacture of soap from kelp. Colonel Gordon of Cluny in Aberdeenshire brought the bankrupt property in 1839 from General MacNeil, who nevertheless went on to have a distinguished career as a soldier.

Colonel Gordon of Cluny, by 1845, had also purchased South Uist and Benbecula and was to gain notoriety for the evictions of thousands of Islanders. He even offered to sell Barra to the Government as a penal colony. Factors and ground officers, aided by the local minister, were responsible for evictions on behalf of the landlord, by recourse to trickery and cruelty.

The formation of the Crofters' Commission and later the Scottish Land Court, brought important changes both in security of tenure and review of rents. In 1900 the Local Government Board bought

The Isle of Barra Hotel

from the Cluny estate some land at Northbay and Eoligarry on which they settled tenant farmers. The government bought the remainder of the island from the Cluny Estate and sold it on in 1939 to the then Chief of the Clan MacNeil, thus returning it after 100 years to MacNeil ownership.

The end of the last century saw a boom in the herring fishing which brought a huge influx of people to the island during the season of May and June. Castlebay was full of sailing fishing boats of 12 – 18 m length, and there were many piers around the bay stacked with barrels for salting herring. Wooden buildings were constructed by the shore to accommodate the gutters and packers who followed the fleet. This prosperity was to disappear as ex-servicemen returned to the depression of the 1920's.

Crofting and fishing, and much tourism in the summer support the people of Barra, and hopefully the processing factory at Ardveenish will continue to give employment.

CULTURE AND ANTHROPOLOGY

The Outer Hebrides have been populated by man for a very long time indeed. It is difficult to say when the first coracle leaked its way across the stormy waters of The Minch, but there is good reason to believe there was a settled community here as early as 5000 BC. There is no evidence to suggest that that particular population was of the well documented Mesolithic hunter gatherer type which occupied the rest of Britain. Indeed they are more likely to have been Neolithic farmers who may have been active at Callanish in Lewis *a full 1000 years* before anywhere else in what is now Britain. Perhaps that was the first of many times the islanders in a totally unsung manner anticipated the mainland. Whoever these people were we now have no way of knowing whether the present day inhabitants are descended from them – but it is interesting to note that the most modern techniques of blood-typing detect strains in the Outer Isles which are unique in Northern Europe and which may well descend from those far off times.

Almost nothing is known of the people who occupied these islands prior to the Norse invasions, which occurred as recently as the 9thC. One of the few names which has survived from before that time appears to be the word 'Lewis' itself in its original form. Its meaning is obscure and (tell it not in Uist) it originally seems to have included in its geographical ambit all the other isles from the Butt of Lewis to Barra Head.

The Nordic Base

The Vikings' occupation was, as one might expect, thorough. There are many things, principally placenames, which remind us of them. They imposed their language and culture on those who had gone before them to such an extent that scholars can only argue interminably on very little evidence whether the autochthonous (earliest known) inhabitants were Celts or non Indo-Europeans.

All major place names of ancient nomenclature are of Norse origin. This is most clearly so in Lewis and becomes more obvious there the further north one goes. Major Norse families emigrated from The Western Isles to Iceland in disgust after the Treaty of Perth (1280) handed over The Western Isles to the neighbouring and savage Kingdom of Scotland, but sufficient of the Norse people must have stayed on as there is evidence to suggest that Norse was spoken in pockets until possibly the 17thC. One reason for so saying is the unchanged nature of so many of the place names.

The mixed ancestry of the Outer Isles had been acknowledged by Gaelic Scotland for centuries and it is in fact reflected in the name which the mainlanders give in Gaelic to the Outer Isles –'Innse Gall', the islands of the strangers. The Gall-Gaels were celebrated (if that is the right word) as being particularly ferocious fighters and were known in English as Gallowglasses, figuring surprisingly large on the English and Irish stages of medieval times.

The Nordic connection can be traced in modern times by direct reference to the physiognomy of many islanders – again with a concentration in the northernmost district of Ness on Lewis, where there is a fairly high proportion of fair haired people standing out quite clearly from the substratum of stockier, darker people, once described as Iberians.

The islanders also have a strong sea going tradition (though that is necessarily common to island folk everywhere) and there are many small day-to-day basic and almost unnoticed habits which are shared with the people of Scandinavia, Faroes and Iceland - such as eating sea fowl (young gannets, fulmars, puffins); making ceann cropaig (fish heads stuffed with fish liver and oatmeal); or eating sgeit gort (skate buried for so long that the ammonia so generated can take one unawares) or sheeps' heads etc. Apart from these gastronomic delights however there is a fair sprinkling of Norse loan words in Gaelic – usually connected with the sea – and, curiously, the Lewis accent bears a remarkably similar intonation pattern to the Norwegian spoken in the Trondheim district of west Norway whence The Western Isles were originally settled.

Nevertheless, despite their long sojourn the Vikings are scarcely remembered in the islands. The principal native clans of MacLeod, Macaulay, Morrison, Maciver and Nicolson (mainly concentrated in Lewis) are of direct Norse descent and while it is true that the chiefs in late medieval days were extremely proud of their Nordic ancestry there is nowadays very little trace of any demotic attempt to make the connection. There are no genuine stories descended to us from the Norse days – and though many stories make reference to these Viking times they are all aetiological in essence. This complete suppression of a real Viking folk tradition also (believe it or not) happened in the Orkney and Shetland Islands – though there a spurious affectation for things Scandinavian has appeared in relatively recent times. One must not forget however that the Nordic connection in the Western Isles was a very large part of the foundation which makes up society in The Western Isles and must always be taken into considerable account despite the apparent apathy with which it is regarded by the present day inhabitants

The Celtic Tradition

This is the tradition which overwhelms the impressionable stranger to begin with – though many things are claimed for it which 'ain't necessarily so'. There is however an Outer Isles flavour which does make our way of life just that little bit different – even from our near neighbours in the Inner Hebrides and mainland Scotland. If you get to know it better you will be able to peel away many layers of differences not at all obvious to begin with which will show that each island and in Lewis each district has a substantial tradition of its own.

Who were/are the Celts? The short answer is that they are a people who first rose to prominence in central Europe about 800 BC. They can truly be described as the very founders of Europe itself. Their civilisation and culture was of a very high level and spread from the centre of the continent out to the extremities including Turkey, Spain and in time the British Isles. All languages have a tendency to change and develop and if isolated to diverge, and proto-Celtic, (a member of the same family as proto-Latin and proto-Greek) was no different. It diverged at a very early date into two basic varieties now called by academics the P and Q Celtic languages. This refers to the fact that one variety tends to change some Q sounds to P and the other does the reverse. These are well known linguistic mutations. Both P and Q Celts reached the British Isles in the centuries after 500 BC. The P Celts are now represented by the Welsh the Cornish and the Bretons (each with their own distinct language as it has now developed) and the Q Celts by the Irish, Scots and the Manx – each again with their own mutually unintelligible languages. If that seems an awful lot of languages, consider how much more fragmented the Teutonic languages (English, High and Low German, Dutch, Scandinavian, etc.) have become.

In Scotland, Gaelic has all but vanished from its traditional half of the country in this century alone. It survives, if only just, in The Western Isles, but it can be scarcely termed healthy even here, despite an average of 75% or so of the population being able to speak it. Recent and frightening statistics show that its use is melting away even more rapidly than anyone feared. Urgent rescue work is being carried out but whether that will be sufficient remains to be seen.

Gaelic is for some a fairly difficult but by no means impossible language to learn, as more and more people are finding out. One problem for a learner amongst Gaels is that the presence or presumed presence of only one English or non-Gaelic speaker in a group will result in all the Gaelic speakers speaking English. This is done out of a courtesy that is certainly misplaced so far as the survival of the language is concerned.

It is probably worth commenting that one of the more famous professors of linguistics reckoned that the Celtic languages had more of the structure of the ideal auxiliary language than any other he knew (Bodmer, *The Loom of Language* 1944) – though that sentiment seems odd given the manner in which the Celtic languages have given way at every turn.

Irish and Scottish Gaelic are really the same language - (as are for instance Danish, Norwegian and Swedish) though the massive support the Irish version gets from that country's Government has no counterpart in Scotland, more's the pity. That is not to say however that Scottish and Irish Gaels are necessarily able to understand one another. Irish Gaelic itself is divided into half a dozen dialects which are not themselves mutually intelligible. As one might expect however, the northernmost Irish dialect is very close to Scottish Gaelic and educated and intelligent Gaels of Donegal and Scotland in general can usually (once they have adapted to the differing rhythms of the two languages) get along not too badly. Scottish Gaelic however has no such divisions on the Irish scale. There are no doubt regional and vocabulary differences which become quite obvious at the extremes of the country – say between Argyll and Lewis – but again an educated Scots Gael (once his ear is attuned) should have no difficulty in conversing the length and breadth of Gaelic Scotland. The less well educated or those with more of a tin ear will no doubt continue to throw up their hands in horror and say that they cannot understand the people of the next island, district or village!

Having got the above general observations out of the way, it is however true to say that there are interesting and real differences in Gaelic as it is spoken in different parts of the Outer Isles themselves. The Island of Lewis (some 850 square miles in extent) is sufficiently large to have several distinct areas within its bounds and these districts (Ness, West Side, Uig, Lochs, (North and South), Back, Stornoway and Point) together with the islands of Harris, North Uist, Benbecula, South Uist, Barra and the different outliers all have vocabulary and idiomatic constructions peculiar to themselves. There are also curious agreements between Barra and Lewis which miss out the islands in between. Much hot air is wasted upon the question of which district speaks the best Gaelic – ie. untainted and uncorrupted by English.

Traditionally Uist Gaelic is very good – but so equally is Uig or Ness Gaelic. Stornoway, Back and Point Gaelic receives most criticism – but curiously enough they seem to be proving slightly more robust since the advent of the TV age. You must remember that television puts an English speaker in the corner of every living room every evening.

The visitor will not at first be able to distinguish between the Gaelic spoken in the different districts and islands, but after a while he or she should be able to distinguish the accents in English as they vary too. There is a quite dramatic isogloss between Harris and Lewis – and though these 'islands' are not geographically distinct there is an absolutely sharp change in the accent over of the boundary line. The great majority of islanders have Gaelic as their mother tongue but apart from Stornoway (centre of anglicisation for centuries) there are increasing numbers of pockets of natives (not just incomers) who are monoglot English speakers. This is particularly true in Benbecula with its overwhelming army presence, but is also found in surprising places – even in Barra and North Uist. This must be very worrying for the supporters of the language but also bodes ill for the way in which English is to be spoken in the future. Traditionally the native Gaelic speaker was formally taught English in school. For that reason his or her English was clear and distinct (if somewhat pedantic) and it could and did take him or her anywhere in the English speaking world. Their descendants without Gaelic however tend to fall into slovenly ways of speech imitated from the mainland.

The following is an example of a traditional Gaelic story of Norse times.

Iomhaigh na Seamraig

A nn an earrainn eile den leabhran seo tha cunntas air a' bhuaidh a bh'aig na Lochlannaich air eachdraidh nan Eilean. Ged is cinnteach tro nan linntean gun deach moran eile dhiubh a chall tha sgeulachdan fhathast ann am beul aithris an t-sluaigh a tha dol air ais gu am nan Lochlannach.

Ann an sgire Nis an ceann a tuath Leodhais cluinnear chun an latha an diugh na facail, "A mhic a' Chruadail!". Bha Cruadal seo a' fuireach air Taobh Thall na sgire o chionn fhada an t-saoghail, agus dithis chloinne aige – caraid mhac, Cailean agus Niall. Air broilleach gach fir bha ceithir spotan dubha agus strianag chaol gan ceangal ri cheile – fior iomhaigh na seamraig cheithir-chluasach.

Ag eirigh suas, be miann Chailein a bhith mun chladach agus iarrtas Neill a bhith an cois a' chruidh air a' mhachair. Thachair aon latha blath bruthainneach gun do thuit Niall 'na throm chadal air an tulaich uaine air an robh e 'na shineadh is an crodh mun cuairt air 'nan laighe anns an fheur is iad a' cnamh an cire. Fhads a bha e 'na shuain co a thainig a nuas bhon chladach ach triuir Lochlannach a bha air a thighinn air tir is iad a' lorg mart a bheathaicheadh sgioba a' bhata aca. Thug iad leo am mart a b'fhearr is Niall bochd comhla ris.

A nis bha Cruadal fhein air basachadh roimhe seo agus chraidh call Neill a mhathair cho gort is gun do chaochail i goirid as a dheidh. Dh'fhag seo Cailean a nis na aonar anns an t-saoghal. Bha e 'na chleachdadh aige a bhith siubhal air feadh na machrach is air barr a' chladaich agus an latha bha seo, is e faireachdainn sgith, nach ann a leig e e-fhein na shineadh air tulach uaine is ann an tiota chaidil e. Thainig thuige ann am bruadar an nighean bu bhoidhche chunnaic e riamh. Chuir i a lamh air ceithir spotan a bhroillich agus ars ise.

'A Chailein Duinn, Mhic thri Chruadail
'S ann air a' chuan a gheibh thu storas;
Nuair a dh'fhalbhas tu ga iarraidh
Thoir do bhrathair Niall a Ronaidh".

Dhuisg Cailean, a' beachdachadh air ailleachd na h-oighe is air na briathran a labhair i. Nuair a thainig e gu aois posaidh shiubhail e fada is farsuing a' lorg te de 'cumadh is de 'boidhcheid. 'S ann an Eilean Bhearnaraidh a thachair e ri te a coltais mu dheireadh, agus cha b'ann ga h-aindeoin a thainig i a Nis comhla ris. Mus do dh'fhag iad Bearnaraidh thug seann bhean ann an sin dha dual a chuireadh e mu amhaich. "Na dealaich ri d'bheo ris," thuirt i, "gus nach bathar air a' mhuir thu's gus nach mortar thu air tir'.

Bha Cailean is a bhean-og gle dhoigheil car uine ach bha iarratas a dh'fheumadh a shasachadh ann an cridhe Chailein a dhol a Ronaidh air toir a bhrathar, Niall. Fhuair e cothrom sin a dheanamh an uair a thainig long a Lochlainn a steach a gheodha air cul an Rudha agus fhads a bha an sgiobha air tir dh'fhalbh Cailean is ceathrar bhalach chalma leatha gu ruigeadh Eilean Ronaidh. Ri fasgadh an eilein bha soitheach Lochlannach eile is an sgioba aice air tir. An an uine nach robh fada bha na Nisich is na Lochlannaich a' cathachadh ri cheile. Mu dheireadh cha robh air fhagail beo ach aon duine air gach taobh, Cailean agus ceannard nan naimhdean.

"Ciod 's ainm dhuit?" arsa Cailean
"Tha Niall," ars am fear eile.
"Fosgail dhomhsa do bhroilleach," thuirt Cailean

Nuair a rinn Niall sin is a chunnaic Cailean na spotan dubha dh'fhosgail e a bhroilleach fhein a' foillseachadh nan spotan ceudna.

"Thugainn dhachaidh," ars esan ri bhrathair
"Ni mi sin," fhreagair Niall

Thill an dithis bhraithrean a Nis le storas mor aca. Bha aoibhneas ann an cridhe Chailein nuair a choinnich e rithist ri mhnaoi - aoibhneas a bh'air a mheudachadh nuair a chaidh innse dha gu robh mac aice bho dh'fhalbh e; mac aig an robh na ceithir spotan dubha air a bhroilleach direach mar a bh'air athair. Co aige tha fios nach eil an sliochd fhathast anns an sgire, agus ma bheir iad suil gheur air am broilleach, nach fhaic iad iomhaigh na seamraig ann an sin.

Gaelic Music

To hear the singing of a Gaelic psalm wafting through the calm of a Hebridean Sabbath evening is an unforgettable experience, transporting the listener back almost to the origins of Gaelic music tradition. The time, given out firstly, line by line by the precentor, is then elongated by the congregation, with the addition of many decorative notes, skillfully interwoven with the melody.

Traditional Gaelic music, in common with folk music in many parts of the world, is mainly built up on the modes of pentatonic scales. This makes it distinct from the music of other parts of Europe.

In The Western Isles, traditional music is currently enjoying a revival and the enthusiastic Lewis and Harris Traditional Music Society brings together musicians from all over the islands. Evenings of combined poetry readings and song; accordion and fiddle groups and dances to traditional music, are all offered by the Society.

The Lewis Pipe Band was first formed in 1904 by a group of local enthusiasts. It has performed at all important island functions, in addition to giving a weekly public performance throughout the Summer months. The band wears the Morrison tartan, in memory of John Morrison, one of its founder members. A pipe band has more recently been formed in Benbecula and is set fair to becoming a similar feature, delighting all those who attend southern isles events.

The Lewis and Harris Piping Society was founded in 1977 to encourage piping, particularly as far as recitals, tuition and competi-

Piping at Feis

tions are concerned. Most of the world's best pipers have graced the stage at the monthly recitals; an annual junior competition for children under 18 is held and children are sponsored to attend competitions throughout the islands and on the mainland. A highly successful summer school was inaugurated a few years ago.

In June of each year, local Mods or musical festivals are held in Lewis, Harris and Uist. Children converge on the Mod venue in their hundreds, to sing, recite and act. Awards are presented at the Grand Concert which follows the competitions and large silver trophies are proudly carried home for a year. In October, individuals and choirs from the islands make their way to the National Mod, held in a different town each year.

In the senior choral section, Stornoway represents the area in the main choral competition from the Lovat and Tullibardine Trophy, while the three rural choirs from Laxdale, Lochs and Tong, vie with one another for the prestigious Lorne Shield. Old acquaintances are renewed and new friends made at this annual gathering of Gaels.

July sees the start of the two week long Barra Festival, started in 1981 by Father Colin MacInnes. This wonderful occasion attracts visitors from all parts of the country and tuition is given in clarsach, fiddle, chanter, guitar, penny-whistle, keyboard, Gaelic singing and conversation and Highland and Hebridean dancing. Ceilidhs are held all over the island and on occasions the historic Castle of Kisimul, strategically situated on a rock in Castlebay harbour, is the evening venue. A smaller festival is held in Lewis, usually in November, with ceilidhs, music workshops and debates, drama evenings and poetry readings. Local artists are backed up by talent imported from the mainland and play to packed houses.

The musical culture of The Western Isles is thriving – proudly preserving its heritage and looking forward with confidence to the future.

CROFTING

A ny visitor to The Western Isles, either driving away from the ferry port or surveying the land from the air will notice the development of houses along the roadside, and in particular a strip of fenced land some two or three hundred metres extending from the house. This is termed a croft.

A croft has been aptly described as a parcel of land entirely surrounded by regulations. It is not an easy concept to describe or for the outsider to understand. With few exceptions most crofts consist of a few acres of arable ground with a proportion of grazing ground shared with other crofts and all must be registered with the Crofter's Commission, a government agency based in Inverness. Each crofter is in simple terms a mini-tenant-farmer – the major distinction being that he has almost absolute security of tenure and can will his croft to a member of his family whether the landlord agrees or not. The croft by the way is the area of ground involved – not the house which is properly termed the 'croft house'. Crofts can vary in size from a quarter of an acre upwards. In Lewis where the crofts are small and relatively unproductive, the average size is probably only about 5 acres. In the Uists where the land is considerably better the acreage is more likely to be 50 or greater. As well as having the sole tenancy of the croft, the crofter usually also has a share in a vast area of 'common grazing' along with other members of his village. Very often the landlord is left with next to nothing 'in hand' save the sporting rights which are however sometimes quite valuable. Over the years the crofter has managed to acquire most of the rights of ownership (plus a few extra) – with few of the disadvantages.

Prior to the 19thC the population of the islands was much smaller than now, the landowners were the chiefs of the people and lived amongst them and nobody's expectations were particularly high. Land was then occupied at the pleasure of the chief – but he was of course the father of the people and their fair treatment was expected and given. Most arable ground in the village was held run-rig – a system which was more or less universal in medieval Europe whereby different strips of arable ground were allocated by lot each year in such a way that everybody got a share of the better and the worse ground in different years. This led however to bad agricultural practices and in time general impoverishment of the arable ground. No one manured the field if he wasn't going to get it next year!

After the very disruptive and confused period following 1745 there was a time of considerable change. The old chiefs sold out to newcomers, the tacksmen (the equivalent of an English squire) emigrated followed closely by many of the clansmen they had abandoned. Rather than continuing with the traditional run-rig system, it became more common for 'crofts' to be laid out. This meant that only one family occupied a parcel of land and tended to improve it.

Just as in other parts of Europe, rural populations were increasing at a vast rate, due in part to the better feeding and diets that were becoming available and improved medical care. The increase in rural population was also in part caused by the desire of the landlords to keep as many people as possible on the land – at least while the kelp and fishing industries were profitable. The fastest growth in the population occurred just at the time when· these labour intensive industries were failing and the new 'improving' landlords were requiring more land for the Cheviot sheep then seen to be the most profitable form of agriculture. Thus commenced the period known as the 'Highland Clearances' which had been going on in Sutherland for a considerable time, and now spread to the islands, where the new improving landlords took full advantage of their legal position to remove the natives from their ancestral grounds. Not all landlords behaved with equal callousness, but history has tarred them all with the same brush.

The people of Lewis fared relatively well under their new proprietor Sir James Matheson. He did however clear at least two areas to create economic farms in Reef and Galson. The cleared crofters were offered alternative land, which in some cases they had to clear for their own use, and some land was open moor which was unsuitable for cultivation. Many, some passage assisted by the proprietor, left for Canada. At least 150 families were sent to Ontario and Quebec in 1851 and as many again in 1863.

The Southern Isles fared much worse at this time and there were large clearances from west and north Harris, Sollas in North Uist, Benbecula and South Uist. Colonel John Gordon, who had bought South Uist and Barra, was prepared to clear the whole Island of Barra and offered the island for use as a convict station to the government. That offer was declined but he got a transportation grant instead and perhaps 2400 people were cleared from these estates and transported to Canada where they were left to their own resources – which were few and caused many to starve. These Barra clearances were carried out in a manner reminiscent of the then current slave hunts on the African Coast. Men were rounded up and handcuffed and those who resisted were held by the press gang. It is understandable why feelings are still readily aroused on the topic of the Clearances. There was not very much that the poor people could do, but with a rapidly increasing population being squeezed into a smaller and smaller area matters were being brought to a head with the potato famine in the 1840s, a further famine in the 1880s (as a result of economic pressures and resultant lack of cash) and over-cropping of poor ground. By themselves it is doubtful whether the crofters would ever have been able to achieve a great deal to improve their position. They

A Barra crofter

were after all very few in number and were not considered at any great length by the government. Their problems however were throughout the 19thC largely paralleled by the much more prominent problems in Ireland.

The famine there of 1879/80 brought into being the remarkable rise of what was called the Irish Land League. The president of the League was one Charles Parnell, then leader of the Irish Party in the House of Commons. The Irish Land Act was passed in 1881 – and this was a marker for what could be achieved in the parallel Highland situation. Very shortly after that pressure began to build for similar treatment to be given to the Highland crofters. There were various direct actions made and taken and a number of confrontations, but at the end of the day, given the decision in Ireland, the justice of the crofter's case could not be denied. The government set up a Crofter's Commission in 1884 under the chairmanship of Lord Napier. The net result of that was the passing of the Crofter's Act of 1886 which, for the first time, gave the crofters security of tenure. The 1886 Act did nothing for the land-less however and that problem was covered in later acts.

It should not be thought that every islander is necessarily a crofter. Crofters nowadays are at the top of their agricultural tree. Their position is to be envied by the many who do not have a croft. There are some people who have no title at all to their homes (squatters) and they are not affected by the crofting acts. Caught as it is in the amber of a mid 19thC solution, the crofting system in the latter half of the 20thC started to show signs of strain. Because the crofters were *only* tenants they were not able to raise funds on their property in the same way as the feuar or owner could. The modern Crofter's Commission duly had the law amended in Parliament and nowadays a crofter can insist upon the purchase of his own house site should he so wish. He can also acquire the croft-land, but that has a complication in that the land remains under crofting tenure which means that subsequent purchasers must still be acceptable to the Commission.

A great deal of money has been spent on agriculture in recent years – largely coming from an Integrated Development Programme (I.D.P.) which was partly (40%) funded by the EC. Over a period of five years from 1981 the programme provided £20 million for agriculture and fish farming and £36 million for infrastructure – such as roads, piers, water and drainage schemes. This injection of capital into the Islands at a period when many parts of Britain were suffering from economic depression did much to support The Western Isles and to put the Island economy onto a much sounder base.

The Development Programme allowed grants to be made to crofters to improve their land, fence in their livestock, and buy new agricultural machinery, though the crofters themselves still had to provide part of the capital and the labour to improve their land. The programme also had a major element of stock improvement and marketing. As you drive around the peaty areas of the Islands it is quite obvious the dramatic change that can result from barren wet peat areas being re-cultivated to green pasture land. These fenced areas of green surrounded by brown are the result of extensive drainage systems, removal of vast amounts of rocks and then re-seeding. Though this form of land reclamation is very expensive, with grant assistance it has allowed the crofting community to improve its land quality, and a co-operative group of crofters such as Lewis Livestock can now export 15000 lambs a year.

Crofting does not normally provide a full income (it never did) but it does give the opportunity to live to a higher standard, and provides the social fabric that holds the population in the Islands.

HARRIS TWEED

The
Harris Tweed
Association
Limited

Certification
Trade Mark

Few visitors to these islands will not have heard of Harris Tweed. The image that the name projects will differ slightly depending on age and social grouping – but a common denominator will be a reputation for high quality craftsmanship.

What then is Harris Tweed? It is a fabric that must be made in The Outer Hebrides, it must be hand woven by the islanders at their own homes – mostly in their small croft houses and it must be made of 100% pure new Scottish wool. Originally the wool was produced entirely within the islands but over the years the wool grown throughout Scotland was recognised as having the same basic qualities and now the wool may originate from anywhere in Scotland. The other processes such as dying, spinning, and finishing must all take place in The Outer Hebrides. If all these things do not happen the product is not entitled to be called Harris Tweed.

How then you may ask did all this come about? The fishermen of the islands had part-time occupations as crofters. While they were at sea following the fish their women folk engaged themselves in making cloth for domestic consumption utilising the wool from their own sheep. Upon shearing each Blackface sheep (or mountain sheep as it was formerly called) produced a fleece of about 3 to 4 pounds in weight. The fleece then had to be washed or scoured. The soft water of the islands was particularly suitable for this purpose but if it was not soft enough a little bran would be added. All the natural grease and all the dirt had to be washed out otherwise the wool would not dye satisfactorily. The next stage was the colouring of the wool – an ancient and artistic craft. It was slow and uncertain but most colours could be obtained from indigenous plants and bushes. The dying process was carried out in the open air generally beside a stream of clear fresh water. A large iron pot was placed over a hot peat fire and the various dying agents were slowly added and an infusion made. Yellow was obtained from rocket and broom, grey and black from iris or oak or alder bark, green from heather, aqua marine from waterlilies and the favourite rusty brown from lichen scraped off the rocks, and known as crotal. Crotal dye was in fact so popular that in the old days it had to be imported from the island of Skye in The Inner Hebrides as so much had been scraped away in the outer islands. The wool was added to the infusion and the pot kept continuously on the boil – perhaps for 24 hours or more. It was then lifted out and washed in fresh water until perfectly clean. Certain colours required the fleece to be washed in salt to preserve its hue.

After washing, the dyed wool was again laid out to dry. Once dry it could then be teased or carded by hand to ensure that all the wool fibres were running in more or less the same direction. At that stage lanolin, to replace the grease removed before dyeing, was added back to the wool – otherwise the cloth would not have any waterproofing. After carding the wool was spun originally on a spindle and whorl but latterly on a spinning wheel. The theory of spinning is simply that fibres arranged longitudinally and then twisted will give a long continuous thread. The yarn required for the warp (the threads which run the length of the web) then had to be arranged in the correct order for the desired pattern. After warping the warp was placed at one end of the loom and threaded through the heddles-wire loops which are lifted in sequence during weaving according to the pattern. Thereafter the cloth was fulled or waulked to be made soft. This used to be done by a team of women beating the cloth on a table to the rhythm of their own Gaelic singing. All these processes were carried out entirely by hand until fairly recently in time. A good housekeeper could produce more cloth than she needed for her own household and the balance was available for sale, or until well into this century, barter.

It is believed that the first full length web of Harris Tweed was sold by the dowager Countess of Dunmore in 1842. She then owned a large part of Harris and took a great interest in her estate. She introduced many of her aristocratic friends to the virtues of Harris Tweed and very soon much of the surplus tweed of that and other islands was gracing the backs of sportsmen and their gamekeepers alike up and down the country. The same cloth of course was made in exactly the same way throughout the whole of the The Outer Hebrides – where it was not known as 'Harris' Tweed but rather more simply as 'clo mor' – or the big or great cloth. Other proprietors following the trend took up the surplus production of their estates and saw to it that it got a market. As the fishing industry declined the menfolk turned their hand to the hard and heavy work of weaving, and so the output of cloth rose and more tweed started to circulate as items of barter in the town of Stornoway. The first person to take commercial advantage of the situation was David Tolmie. He had contacts in the London markets and started the first business offering island tweed on a regular commercial basis, instead of the personal, aristocratic and somewhat haphazard basis of the previous 50 years. Other Stornoway entrepreneurs speedily saw their opportunity and within an extremely short time the industry was organised and competitive.

A weaver at his loom

Demand was so greatly stimulated by Royal and other patronage over the first decade of this century that demand considerably exceeded supply and speedier ways of carrying out the ancillary processes were developed by some of the bigger producers. Machine carding for a small percentage of yarn was introduced, followed by a tolerable proportion of mill dyeing, spinning and finishing. Without a doubt these were improvements which allowed quality control, pattern repeats, and all the other requirements of a modernising industry to be imposed – and yet they did not interfere with the independence of the crofter/weaver who was weaving the cloth still in his own home far away from the spinning and finishing mills. On 9th December 1909 a protective agency representing the major interests in the infant industry was set up calling itself the Harris Tweed Association Ltd (H.T.A.). Its first act was to apply for a standardisation mark from the Board of Trade. This and the name Harris Tweed were granted to the HTA, described officially as a body for the protection of the Harris Tweed Industry – the owners of the famous Orb trade mark. The Orb originated in the Coat of Arms of the Countess of Dunmore who had done so much for the whole idea in the 1840s and 1850s.

As well as promoting the industry the H.T.A. also polices it. Their inspectors check on both the mills and the weavers and will not stamp the cloth with the famous mark unless they are satisfied that it conforms in every respect with the conditions laid down in the trade mark. This also provided one of the first forms of consumer protection, the industry with this umbrella of protection developed continuously over the next half century or so. The biggest change was the introduction in the 1920's of the Hattersly loom by Lord Leverhulme – a much more efficient piece of apparatus allowing the craftsman to create more adventurous patterns, with much greater accuracy. The motive power for the Hattersly loom is still the weaver himself, through pedals which drive the shuttles and change the heddles. These looms are the weaver's own property and are kept at the weaver's homes – usually in small sheds. Each weaver is still entirely self-employed – for, though most of the rest of the processes are now carried out by mills for the whole of the islands, the actual weaving is still carried out by the independent crofter – weaving sometimes for one mill, sometimes another. In this way the Harris Tweed industry has assisted the indigenous population to remain which otherwise may long since have been scattered. There are now approximately 750 independent weavers and about 400 millworkers. A weaver is a craftsman – some can be described as full-time and can produce three webs of tweed a week, each measuring some 80 to 90 yards in length. Others are part-time and still engage in supplementary fishing or croft work and may only do one tweed a week or even a fortnight. The cloth is limited in width by the physical operation of the treadle loom to the traditional 28/30 inch single width cloth.

The industry produces approximately 5 million yards of tweed per annum (depending upon demand) which is sold all over the world. There are still three basic weights of tweed now produced – standard weight (the original heavy tweed), the light, and the feather or bantam weights much more suited to city life. A huge selection of patterns of every conceivable hue are sent out every year to agents all over the world but the traditional patterns seem to remain the most popular. As well as the big mills there still remain a few small producers of the old style, carrying on business in a minor way. Twenty years ago there were a multitude. The different mills and producers are in competition the one with the other all the time all over the world. The American market has been traditionally the most important, but other markets have been developed over the years to attempt a wider more balanced approach. As it is, the industry is subjected to cyclical swings of popularity as tweed goes in or out of fashion.

The industry has always to be on its toes to detect imitators and pirates throughout the world – and that is in truth a matter of survival for the whole community. Despite the inter-firm rivalry already mentioned, the Harris Tweed industry is again unique in that it spends a fair proportion of its advertising revenue each year on corporate advertising via the Harris Tweed Association Ltd. The funds for this are raised from the industry by means of a levy imposed on each yard of tweed presented for stamping with the Orb mark. This stamp is applied every three yards to the reverse of the tweed after it

48

has been finished and is the guarantee that the tweed has been entirely made from pure virgin wool produced in Scotland, dyed, spun and finished in The Outer Hebrides and hand woven at his own home by an islander. The H.T.A. as well as funding the corporate advertising also spends a great deal of time policing, inspecting and helping all the different parts of the industry. There is a staff engaged full time in this task. As well as that domestic policing the H.T.A. is continually registering its Trade Marks as they appear to be required or as they lapse throughout the world, and is nearly always in litigation somewhere or other against pirates, who know a good thing to copy if they can get away with it. The H.T.A. continually find emergent countries which see the industry as one to emulate and see nothing wrong with renaming a local weaver's village, 'Harris' for example. That is usually quite easily dealt with – if expensively, but constant vigilance is the price which has to be paid for relative success. In world-wide textile terms the Harris Tweed Industry is not even a flea bite but it is of immense importance here, and is very, very well known.

As you tour round the island you will frequently hear the 'click-clack' of the looms, and see the woven tweeds lying at the gates of the crofts waiting to be collected by the mill lorries for finishing and dispatch to the far corners of the globe. Harris Tweed thankfully remains a unique fabric in a world of increasing uniformity and mass production.

THE FISHING INDUSTRY

There is no doubt that the indigenous industry of the Western Isles is fishing. Despite the present diversification of employment through the Harris Tweed Industry and such as the fitful and transient oil industry related yard at Arnish, the service industries and now fish farming, the activity which goes back through the centuries is fishing. Dean Munro, in 1549, referred to fishing with a rod and a large net for whiting, hake and haddock. In 1594 the Dutch appeared off the coast of Lewis having been given a licence by King James VI which permitted them to fish outside a limit of 28 miles and, in very early times, the fishing around The Western Isles was worked by the French and Spanish. The pressure by King James VI on the Fife Adventurers (*see* page 12-13) was largely due to the expected profit he hoped to make out of the Minch fisheries. This explained his extreme annoyance at their failure.

Fishing has been, for at least five hundred years, the single most important commercial activity of The Western Isles. The earliest form of commercial fishing by the islanders was in open boats powered by 4 oars, and using small lines which consisted of four 'strings' each about 42 metres long with 500 baited hooks. Longlines were made of heavier cord, and the boats used in longline fishing were between 6 and 8 metres long. Longlines were left out for 48 hours or more.

It was in the early 18thC that the islanders took to commercial fishing in earnest, with fish merchants engaging crews to fish exclusively for them before the season started, with an arrangement to purchase all their fish at a stipulated price. All the fish merchants kept stores in which all kinds of goods were sold (not only those for fishing purposes). The merchants expected the fishermen, who were in debt to them, or whom they engaged to fish for them, to purchase from their stores.

Before the arrival of the fish merchants crews such as those on Barra used to cure their own catch and transport it to the Clyde, in exchange for goods and clothing. On Lewis the Factor and Tacksmen contracted with their tenants to fish for them, and provided boats and tackle for that purpose. There was plenty of fish in the Minch from Stornoway to Barra Head and in Loch Roag, so the fishermen did not have to go too far out to sea in their sailing boats.

The herring fishery really began in the early 18thC, when cargoes of herring were sold to Inverness from Stornoway. There was, however, a decline in the herring fishery towards the end of the 18thC due to over-fishing – a problem not unknown in the present day. The failure of the herring fishery eventually led the menfolk to follow the

Stornoway Harbour

fishing to the east coast and subsequently they were followed by the women who, by the 1860's, were to be found in every fishing port between Peterhead and Lerwick and south to Great Yarmouth.

The peak of the herring fishing at the end of last the century saw Castlebay and Stornoway harbours filled with almost a thousand fishing boats each, with jetties projecting in all directions surrounded by boats and covered with barrels. This was the heyday of the 'Zulu' fishing vessels, so named as they appeared at the time when the South African War had been concluded. The 'Zulu' carried enormous sails, usually coloured brown and reaching up to 25 metres high.

Money had been loaned by the Fishery Board to fishermen in the crofting areas around the turn of the century for the purchase of new and second-hand boats. Many of the sailing boats were converted into motor boats in the early part of the 20thC. Steam drifters became very common as the century progressed, but the herring and white fishing industries gradually declined, chiefly due to illegal trawling by fishermen from east coast ports.

Following the 1914-18 war and particularly the Russian revolution of 1917 the Baltic markets for fish, which were the main ones, were lost and unemployment rose, with emigration being the result of the failure of the schemes for the promulgation of fishing envisaged by Lord Leverhulme. Indeed, following the departure of Lord Leverhulme in 1924, such fishing as there was failed, thus casting doubt on whether his schemes would have in any event succeeded. Following the 1939-45 war the government established the White Fish Authority, the Herring Industry Board and in 1964, the Highlands and Islands Development Board. For some years immediately after the 1939-45 war there had been some success in the herring fishery, with the fish being kippered and salted for export. Indeed, when the Queen visited Stornoway in 1956 she was shown a curing station for herring on South Beach Quay, and was presented with a 'cutag' or gutting knife. Shortly after that however the Stornoway fleet dwindled, until assistance had to be given by the Macaulay Trust and latterly by the Highlands and Islands Development Board.

There were considerable landings of herring up until 1977, when the Minch was closed for herring fishing due to the depletion of stocks. Prior to 1977 the herring were being purchased by Norwegian and Faroese Companies who were operating 'klondyking' operations. The term 'klondyking' means that the fish are being purchased from local fishermen by other fishing interests who do not fish the waters themselves.

The fishing industry in The Western Isles now employs around 1050 people, of which some 500 are classed as regularly employed fishermen, about 170 are part-time or crofter-fishermen and about 350 are employed in ancillary activities such as processing and marketing. There are about 376 vessels now engaged in the industry, although 300 of these are under 10m, and the main fishing effort today is concentrated on shellfish, which accounts for about 80% of landings by value. The main species caught are nephrops (prawns), lobsters, crab and scallops, while the catch of white fish is mainly confined to the incidental by-catch of the nephrop fishery.

Western Isles Fish Landings (£ million)

	1975	1994
Demersal (Whitefish)	0.3 (17%)	1.36 (12.9%)
Pelagic	0.84 (50%)	0.005 (0.04%)
Shellfish	0.56 (32%)	9.17 (87.04%)
TOTAL	**1.70**	**10.54**

Source: DAFS

'Active' fishing vessels by area
(1994)

Loch Roag
Lobster & crab creeling and netting for dogfish based in Kirkibost (mainly) & Carloway

3

Seasonal crab fishery by one or two vessels

2

ATLANTIC

OCEAN

L E W I S

M I N C H

1

Stornoway
Mainly prawn trawlers and crab

4

H A R R I S

Scalpay
Prawn trawling – prawn creeling – scallop dredging

5

6

Berneray
Lobster & velvet crab

7

Leverburgh/ Rodel

NORTH UIST

8

T H E

Kallin
(Grimsay)
Winter fishing for prawns & velvet crab (creel caught)

BENBECULA

9

10

West side of Uist only accessible to small local vessels during *summer*. Developing dogfish fisheries

S O U T H   U I S T

11

Eriskay/Ludag
(South Uist)
Creel vessels – crab, lobster etc

12

BARRA

13

Castlebay
Mainly creel vessels – but also prawn trawling & scallop dredging

Lewis & Harris	
Area	*Number of boats*
1 Stornoway	27
2 Broadbay – Ness	34
3 West Side	30
4 Lochs	22
5 Scalpay	27
6 Harris	39
Total	179
Uists & Barra	
7 Berneray	8
8 North Uist	36
9 Grimsay	28
10 Benbecula	15
11 South Uist } 12 Eriskay	47
13 Barra & Vatersay	63
Total	197
Western Isles TOTAL	**376**

Source: Fisheries Office, Stornoway

The table above gives the landings for 1975 and 1994 and shows both the growth of the shellfish catch and the dramatic decline in the traditional pelagic catch – particularly herring – over the last few years.

The waters around The Western Isles were amongst the richest fishing grounds in Europe but with the over-fishing which has taken place in other areas such as the North Sea, there has been a steady increase in the number of large vessels fishing in the Minches and to the west of the Islands in recent years, which has quite dramatically reduced the inshore catches for small boat owners. Unfortunately The Western Isles fleet is showing its age in terms of fuel efficiency, adaptability and catching capacity at a time when regulations permit larger and more efficient vessels from other areas of Scotland (and soon from the rest of Europe) to fish the same grounds. This has resulted in a decline in earnings for Western Isles fishermen and their inability to invest in the new boats which are required to exploit existing resources more efficiently, and to develop new fisheries.

Although the EC funded Integrated Development Programme (1982-1987) succeeded in improving harbour and landing facilities – eg. Scalpay; Kirkibost, Gt Bernera; Kallin, Grimsay; also Grimishader, North Uist; Polnacrann, Benbecula and Orosay, South Uist – and encouraged processing and marketing developments throughout the Islands, no EC funds were made available under the Programme for the modernisation of the fishing fleet.

There is very little white fish landed in The Western Isles, and what is landed is either sold locally, or gets shipped to Aberdeen – prices being low here due to the cost of transportation. The fleet relies primarily on shellfish. The trawl fleet, based mainly in Stornoway, lands mostly prawn 'tails' which supply local processors. Scallop dredging has been on the increase in recent years (the detrimental effect of this method on a variety of stocks could be felt soon), but the biggest growth sector has been creeling, based at the smaller ports. During 1994 creel caught shellfish, comprising mainly nephrops, lobsters, brown crabs and velvet crabs was worth £4.05 million. Trawl landings of nephrops and white fish were worth £4.35 million. There is no processing on the islands, with everything (except the white fish) being shipped live to France and Spain. Ten truck-loads leave the islands each week.

Lobster, the mainstay of the Loch Roag and Uist (Griomsaigh) fleets in previous years is steady, but stocks are under increasing pressure. This is a 'live' trade – geared to higher value export markets with no processing impact. However the pressure upon stocks has lead the development of netting and lining for species such as dogfish and turbot.

There has been a general trend towards co-operation in marketing by fishermen in recent years. Stornoway now has a well established

Processing plants

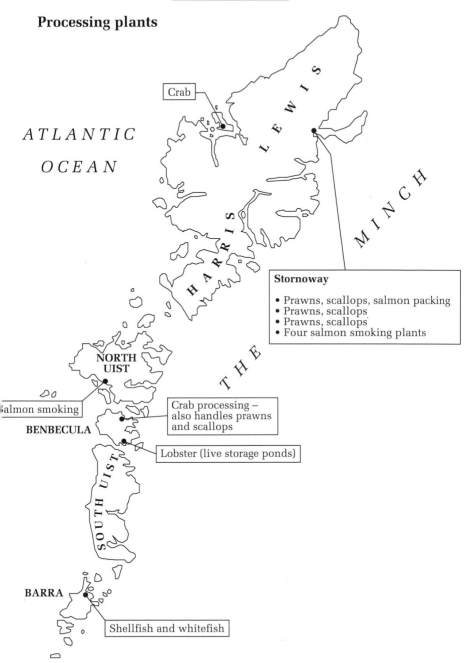

Fishermans Co-operative, and the South Uist Fish Marketing Co-operative has been recently formed with assistance from the Integrated Development Programme, set up with EEC money.

FISH FARMING

The modern practice of fish farming started with trout on fresh water lochs and has now developed into a major industry. Salmon farming started in the early 1960's and soon the potential of the clear unpolluted waters of The Western Isles was appreciated, and in 1988 The Outer Hebrides produced and sold 236 tonnes of Atlantic salmon, and 100 tons of shellfish valued at £8.5 million.

Initially the large funds required to set up fish farms meant that only multinational companies or the large estates could afford to try this new venture. In 1982 the European Economic Community (EEC) made available £20 million for agriculture and fish farming, in an Integrated Development Programme. The number of local people who were prepared to take a chance with their money, time and sheer hard work in order to participate in and develop a new industry for their islands was quite surprising. With the exception of the construction yard at Arnish on Lewis, fish farming is the first new industry to come to The Western Isles this century.

Island people have for generations sailed over every ocean and to every corner of the world in merchant ships, warships, whalers and trawlers. So it is not surprising that people with the sea so deeply inbred would take the opportunity of involving themselves in an industry that allowed them the concept of farming the sea. The industry now employs about 300 people full time and 70 part time, many being self-employed and owning their own fish farm. There is also an increasing number of people employed in gutting, packing, smoking, marketing and transporting the produce, as the small farms combine to promote their excellent fish. One excellent spin-off has arisen with the haulage contractors, who can now reduce their charges for goods coming to the islands, as their lorries now have a full load to return with, which again helps the local economy.

As you travel around the islands you may well notice long, low lying buildings beside streams – these are the salmon hatcheries. The salmon eggs have to be hatched and reared in fresh water, and again the island water is particularly suited to the rearing of juvenile salmon right through from fry to parr, and finally to smolt, the final stage before being introduced into sea water.

In April each year the hatcheries transfer that year's crop to sea water cages, transporting the smolts in water tanks either by road or sea, although recently the use of a helicopter has made the process much more successful. In most of the sheltered sea lochs fish cages can be seen; they are square in shape with a floating pontoon around the edges supporting a net in the middle. Even from some distance the salmon can be seen leaping from the surface. The smolts are kept

A typical fish farm

in the cages for one year until they are grilse, the maturing salmon, which would normally wish to return to the river they were hatched in. The harvesting of the salmon has to be done efficiently and quickly. The internal temperature of the fish must be reduced to 2°C within a matter of minutes if the high quality of the fish is to be maintained.

Experimentation is still continuing in farming more shellfish and white fish, and the clear water and sheltered lochs of The Western Isles will certainly see an increase in this attractive new industry.

RELIGION

The Western Isles is basically a very religious community which has evolved into a Roman Catholic minority dominant from Benbecula southwards and a subdivided Calvinist protestant majority dominant from Benbecula northwards. Perhaps because each section is dominant and secure in its own geographical unity there has been little confrontation of the kind that is all too often evident in other parts of the world and religion is simply not an issue between islanders when they meet. Nevertheless the different churches have very strong views on their own religion and very different perspectives of the religious past of these islands and so this chapter is a compilation of observations given by the major denominations.

Prehistory

Nothing at all is known of the religious beliefs of those islanders who built the Callanish Stone Circle in Lewis – or the other circles dotted around the islands. They are often referred to as 'Druidical remains' – but of course they predate, by perhaps 2500 years, the druids who did not arrive on these shores until the Celts came around 500 BC. Many researchers now believe the stone circles were more celestial and seasonal calendars rather than temples. Of the druids if they ever operated in the islands one can only guess at what they believed in though a few odd superstitions which lingered on in different parts of the island until late medieval or early modern times may possibly trace back to these days – but nothing now survives.

The Coming of Christianity

The start of Christianity in The Western Isles is a very misty area where it is difficult to be too definite, but was probably introduced after the coming of St Columba from Ireland in 563 AD. St Columba introduced Irish monks to the western seaboard, and although it is not known whether he himself came to The Outer Hebrides at any point, it is certain that his fellow missionaries did in considerable numbers. The names of islands and townships bear witness to their presence. On the island of North Rona is probably the earliest Christian building and evidence of other buildings was found on remote islands such as Sula Sgeir, the Flannans and the Shiants. Norse names such as Pabbay – Priest island and Bayble – Priest village are common throughout the Islands.

It is believed that the Hebrides got their first bishop about the

The interior of St Moluag's Church at Eoropie in Ness

year 838, using the title of the Bishopric of Sudreys or Southern Isles, but as the Norse were then in control of these islands and were basically pagan until the 11thC, the Church's influence must have been limited. In 1098 the Bishopric of Sudrey and Man were placed under the authority of Ragnald, Bishop of Trondheim in Norway where they remained until as late as 1380. During this period missionary priests were sent from Uig, in Lewis, to Iceland. Indeed Islivig, in Brenish is named after Bishop Isli who was active in converting Iceland.

An interesting relic of the Norse Christian period is the little chapel of St Olav in Gress Cemetery named after a Norwegian Saint – King Olav. Also with Norse connections we still have St Moluag's Church at Eoropie in Ness, now in Episcopalian care and beautifully restored. It is built in the Norse style of the 12th and 13thC. Dr W. Douglas Simpson, the antiquarian, says that "There can be no doubt that in Teampull Mholuidh we must recognise a church founded or re-established on a Celtic site about the end of the 12thC, under the patronage of some Norse or Celto–Norse chief in Lewis. Clearly the building was of exceptional importance. It possessed a famous sanctuary, and perhaps it is not without significance that in local tradition it is styled 'The Cathedral'". The St Moluag for whom it is named was one of the great Irish missionaries and a contemporary of St Columba.

The Norse of the islands retained some of their pagan superstitions after they had, officially at least, embraced Christianity. There is a rich history of fact and legend about some of the many Christian foundations and healing wells in the Islands. Lewis and Harris alone are known to have some thirty chapels, religious houses and healing wells. Some are pin pointed on a map exhibited in the porch of the Roman Catholic church in Stornoway.

From the 12thC until the reformation of 1560 information is rather scant, though there are remains of several ecclesiastical structures. Cille Bharra may have been built or rebuilt around the 12thC and though it fell into ruin during the 16thC it has been rebuilt and is still in use.

In Benbecula, Nunton or Baile na Cailleach, there certainly appears to have been a convent which was in ruins by the 17thC and of which there is now very little remaining though there are many local tales of its demise.

In Rodel, South Harris, is the famous St Clement's church, a priory built about the 13thC, probably on an earlier site, and restored about 1500 by Alexander MacLeod with stone from Mull similar to that used in the Construction of Iona Abbey. The Chiefs of the MacLeods of Harris, now styled MacLeod of MacLeod with their seat in Skye, were buried within the Church and an effigy of Alexander MacLeod sculpted in 1528 can be seen today.

The other earlier priory was attached to the church of St Columba at Ui (Aignish, Lewis) and what remains now on the original 6thC site is a 14thC chapel enlarged to its present size about 1500 AD. The ruins are now well kept and the graveyard is the burial ground for the MacLeod chiefs of Lewis, and of the MacKenzies of Seaforth.

During the post reformation period from 1560 onwards there was a gradual change from the old Roman Catholic faith to the Protestant faith.

It is often thought that the Protestant Reformation never reached south of Benbecula, but that is not exactly true as the Roman Catholic priests were expelled and some of the MacNeil chiefs of Barra immediately after the reformation were Protestant. There were attempts to establish Presbyterian and Episcopalian churches, but the islands were to all intents abandoned by religious authority. Visiting Catholic missionaries To Barra in the 17thC found there was still a following for their patron saint, St Finnibar, and were able to revive the original Catholic faith, which despite several attempts at conversion by the Protestant churches, has remained very firm to the present day.

The Patronage act of 1712 allowed a landlord the right to nominate the parish minister. Some landowners such as the Honourable Mrs Stewart Mackenzie, daughter of the last Earl of Seaforth, actively supported the Church and the spreading of the gospel and brought the evangelical minister, Mr Alexander MacLeod, to Lewis but others paid little attention. The introduction of schooling to teach people to read the Gaelic Bible resulted in 1822 in a religious revival which took place mainly in Barvas and Uig. This strong wave of religious fervour swept through the islands. The problem of lay patronage did not go away naturally however and in 1843 a third of Scottish Ministers walked out of the established Church of Scotland to form the Free Church of Scotland, because the state would not change the law on the issue. The majority in Lewis 'came out' with the Free Church because it seemed to them to represent the cause of vital evangelical Christianity in Scotland. The dissenting ministers had to leave their manses and churches and preach in the open air. Within a year only one Free Church Minister remained on the island, but the members with their uncompromising commitment to Sacred Principles continued their worship with lay leaders. Well known Free Church Ministers were brought from the mainland to help spread the gospel in the remoter areas. Within fifteen years of the disruption there were eight large Free Church congregations in Lewis.

The Free Presbyterians maintain a wholehearted allegiance to the Westminster Confession of Faith, and follow vigorously the basic principles of the great Protestant Reformers Calvin and Knox.

In 1893 a second disruption occurred in the highlands, this time within the Free Church of Scotland itself when two ministers, both from North Uist and preaching one in Raasay and one in Sheildaig, protested over a Declaratory Act and seceded from the Free Church of Scotland and formed the Free Presbyterian Church.

The 'established' or state Church of Scotland, which is also Presbyterian in Government, is of course still very much in evidence throughout the islands.

The present Free Church dates from 1900 when the majority of congregations in the Free Church of Scotland and the United Presbyterian Church united to form the United Free Church of Scotland, but a large proportion of people in Lewis were against this union and the largest congregations 'continued' as the Free Church of Scotland, being popularly referred to as the 'Wee Frees'. The United Free Church was later to join with the Established Church of Scotland in 1929.

Religion Today

The Western Isles has now been left with five traditional denominations (see diagram on page 62) – the Salvation Army, as well as small groups of Muslims, Mormons and Baha'i and others. Religious beliefs, it may be seen, play a very important part in the present way of life.

Barra, Eriskay, South Uist and part of Benbecula have a community spirit which is led and dominated by the local Roman Catholic Priests, who work hard and contribute greatly to the morale and standards of their parish. Their Sabbath while still observed is certainly

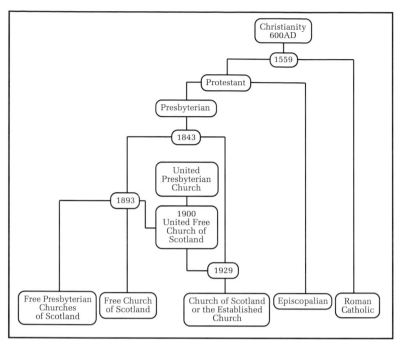

more relaxed than that of North Uist, Lewis and Harris, and it is much more acceptable for the visitor to travel about, and even to watch the many organised games of football in the afternoon.

In the Presbyterian Churches the role of the minister is perhaps not as pastoral as that of the priests, but he is seen more as a teacher and an interpreter of the scripture. The religious picture seen in Lewis and Harris is not thought to be as a result of the collective personal powers of the ministers but rather as a result of the congregations' interpretation of the Word of God.

Sabbath Observance is held most strictly in Lewis and Harris. All churches welcome visitors to their congregations. The Lord's day is upheld in traditional manner more than in any other part of Britain, and visitors should be aware that for most locals travelling is kept to a minimum and all normal bus and transport services and facilities are suspended during Sunday.

Visitors attending a Free Church or Free Presbyterian service will find a church with no trappings or ornaments, a very simple central pulpit, no organ music but a 'precentor' leading the congregation in Psalm singing.

Devout Presbyterians of the three denominations can enjoy church meetings not only twice on Sunday but about every evening of the week as well. The mid-week services are prayer meetings and in the rural areas each small community without a church may well have a meeting hall. The visitor may often see a small shed-like building with a long line of cars parked on the verge. The services at these meetings are often well attended and, to the frequent surprise of the outsider, often with a high proportion of lively young people.

In contrast with the situation which obtains in some other churches where first communion is taken as an adolescent, to become a full communicant member of the Presbyterian churches requires a full and proper commitment and a full confession of faith. Some otherwise regular attenders feel not always able to give this full commitment (often enough from a feeling of not being good enough) and remain as 'adherents' of the Church.

The time of Communion is twice a year, usually in the Spring and Autumn, and the same weekend is used by all three presbyterian denominations in each village. The entire weekend is regarded as a holy time starting on the Wednesday evening to the Monday evening and some shops and transport services are curtailed during Thursday, Friday and Saturday. The communion 'season' extends over several weeks as each area has its own weekend and many members travel to different areas to join in their services which are usually officiated by visiting ministers.

THE WESTERN ISLES TODAY

The Western Isles are unique within the British Isles not only for their variety of landscape and their wealth of interest to the naturalist and historian, but more especially for their Gaelic culture. To many of the islanders Gaelic is their first language – to the very old and very young it is their only language – though unfortunately radio and television have taken their inevitable toll on general usage. Comhairle nan Eilean (the Western Isles Islands Council) now has a bilingual Policy and is doing much to maintain the use of Gaelic. There is an increase in Gaelic radio and television programmes, but not nearly enough to help the language prosper. The Gaelic culture has remained prominent more so in The Outer Hebrides than in any other part of Scotland, and the way of life and philosophy of the islanders gives it a charm and fascination that will intrigue visitors.

The Western Isles is not a remote backwater, but a community surviving against enormous social and economic changes. Male unemployment in 1994 was 27%, yet we do not find ourselves with poverty or vast social problems. Apart from Stornoway many of the prices for goods and services are at least 20% more than that of the mainland. It may also surprise visitors to see the vast number of new houses and cars. These should not be taken as a sign of wealth, but considered in conjunction with the people's priorities and outlook on life, and the type of employment and financial assistance received.

Apart from the few main farming areas on the islands there are not the same number of large stone houses built at the beginning of this century that can be seen on Skye, Mull or Tiree, but new houses built during the past twenty years with grant aid. Most of the houses seen along the roadside are 'croft houses', that is, houses belonging to crofts. 'Croft houses', if they had to be rebuilt, were eligible for a grant and a loan from the Department of Agriculture. This financial assistance did not cover the cost of the house, but by using local tradesmen and undertaking a lot of the work themselves crofters have been able to provide good quality housing. Many of the older houses have also been completely renovated with the assistance of Local Authority Improvement Grants.

The islanders are basically hard working people who spend a lot of time trying to improve their homes and crofts. Leisure activities are almost unheard of for the older generations and holidays are rare, except for the occasional trip to the mainland for shopping or to visit relatives. The external appearance of the house or croft is not considered to be of vital importance – as can be seen by some of the rather untidy sights around the islands.

Stornoway, the only town on The Western Isles

The interiors of the houses are usually clean, tidy and well decorated. As in many rural areas the main room of the house is the kitchen and it is usually large, accommodating a table, chairs, armchairs and a large stove used for cooking and heating. Outside most houses you will see large stacks of peat, or 'cruachs'. These can even be found in the town of Stornoway. Peat is one of the main sources of domestic fuel used on the islands, and every spring sees the start of the peat cutting ritual. This is very often a family affair, with one person cutting the peat using a 'tairisgean' (a wooden handled iron cutting tool and spade) to cut the slabs of peat out of the bank, the other person catching and throwing them carefully onto the surrounding moor. The peat is left to dry, turned over, and then stacked in small piles to dry completely before being taken home. The gathering of the peats is a communal activity with groups of relatives and friends – even whole village communities – carting the bags of peats to the roadside, loading them into trailers, then stacking them at the side of the houses. Even though it is sometimes a backbreaking process for six or seven days, the saving of the cost of a whole year's fuel supply for heating and cooking makes it well worthwhile.

Throughout The Western Isles there are about six thousand crofts, of which four thousand will have animals – mostly sheep. Many of the crofters will also have other jobs such as fishing or weaving, or be employed full time. The standard of crofts has greatly improved since the Integrated Development Programme of the EEC was introduced, with many areas being drained and re-seeded and new stock and equipment being purchased. The formation of cooperatives to market their produce has also revitalised crofting.

The Harris Tweed Industry now counts for about 750 jobs on Lewis and Harris, of which seven hundred and fifty are self-employed weavers working from their own homes, some of whom are also crofters. The fishing industry has declined dramatically since the beginning of this century, but there is now an increase in the number of static gear fishermen; these are generally smaller boats fishing for shellfish, and the ever increasing fish farming industry giving a total of about 900 jobs. In the Uists one of the main employers is the Army, which has its headquarters on Benbecula. As well as employing staff for maintenance services and secretarial duties, the Army has offered apprenticeship schemes for young people in several trades.

Comhairle nan Eilean (The Western Isles Islands Council) has three offices, the largest being in Stornoway, with smaller offices in Balivanich and Castlebay. Although government cut-backs have resulted in a reduction in their labour force, they still employ a total of 1,350 full time and 930 part-time staff, including 860 education staff based in the various schools throughout the islands.

The Lewis Offshore construction yard, based at Arnish on Lewis is locally owned and employs about 200 people, although employment in this volatile industry depends on orders available. Tourism as yet is not a major industry, even though many of the islanders cater for bed and breakfast visitors during the summer months.

The creation in 1974 of Comhairle nan Eilean (Western Isles Islands Council) has meant a polarisation towards Stornoway from the mainland of many of the administrative headquarters of various organisations. One result has been a more understanding treatment of functions and problems throughout the islands than was achieved under the previous mainland centres. Those in the southern isles may feel they are far removed from the decision making, but increasingly senior administrative and professional jobs are being undertaken by island people, who have an intimate knowledge of the community. For many years the islands had a reputation for producing scholars who, after university education, were unable to find employment in their own community, but now more suitable and responsible positions are slowly becoming available.

If one travels north through The Western Isles, Stornoway may almost seem out of place, with an urban framework not found elsewhere in the islands. The hustle and bustle around the town centre is enough to make the country visitor wish to leave and return to tranquillity as soon as possible. As it is the only town on The Western Isles it is much busier than any mainland town of 8,000 inhabitants, as many people commute from all corners of the island, and unfortunately for the visitor the limited bus service is geared to bring people from the rural areas to the town in the morning and travel from the town to the country in the evening.

Harris, the outlying edges of Lewis, North Uist, Barra and Eriskay have not changed as dramatically this century as have Stornoway and Benbecula. The influx of the army to Benbecula has considerably altered part of the island. The Royal Artillery Range Hebrides, including Royal Air Force Benbecula, provides a community of about 700 people – troops and their families. There are also a number of ex-forces personnel who have settled on Benbecula, as well as civilians indirectly connected to the range activities. On one side there has been an effect on the culture of the island, especially in the schools where the predominance of English speaking children outnumber the native Gaelic speakers, but most of the army personnel treat the area as an overseas posting, remaining very much self-contained, and although enjoying the freedom of the area they do not mix a great deal with the locals.

On the other hand the range has provided a considerable boost to employment, as well as providing sixteen apprenticeships in engineering each year and employment under various government youth training schemes. The range also shares some of its sporting facilities, its medical services and provides emergency ambulance cover for Benbecula. Because of the presence of the range there has been extra financial assistance with the building of the local school and causeway. The continual movement of troops, equipment and families has also ensured a regular air and sea service for the islands.

The function of the Royal Artillery Range Hebrides is purely to allow regiments of the Army and Royal Air Force the opportunity to practice firing their missile armament in complete safety. There is no experimental or strategic importance to the range. The Royal Air Force has almost 100 personnel in a new compound in Balivanich. Their role is the radar surveillance of the western approach to northern Europe, and the control of military aircraft within that area, and as such does have some strategic importance.

TRACING YOUR ROOTS
IN THE WESTERN ISLES

Many of the visitors to the Islands come in order to try to trace their roots. Some come with fully researched pedigrees, and some with a vague idea that they had a relative who was a MacLeod. And of course, some are successful in tracing ancestors and relatives, and others not. So, it might be useful to the visitor to give some ideas of what you should do before starting searching here, and some of the resources that are available here in the Islands.

The first thing is to realise that the islands have a population of about 30,000, and about half of them *share the same five surnames.* So it is important to have as much information as possible before you arrive here. If you have the name and approximate age of the person who left the Islands, and a rough idea of when they left, that is a big help, as is whether they were married then or not. Do you know where they settled first when they left here? Did they call their new home by an Island name? What were the names of the first genera-tion of children?

If your people left the Islands this century, and you know from which village, then the task of tracing your relatives should be fairly easy. In almost every village there is someone, usually elderly, who has a command of all the families in the area. This source is so obvi-ous that it is often overlooked, but it is so much the best source that it should always be tried. After all, you could well be talking to someone who remembers your people personally.

If there is no local expert, then check whether there is a Comuinn Eachdraidh – Historical Group – working in the area. Currently there are Comunn Eachdraidh working in Ness, Barvas, Carloway, Uig and Lochs in Lewis, in Tarbert, Harris, and in the Uists and Barra. These are groups set up to gather in local information, often from oral sources, and most of them have been gathering records of families also. There is the additional bonus with most Comuinn Eachdraidh that they are also gathering old photographs, and you might even come across a photograph of some of your own family – there was a case when we were completely stuck with a family, until the visitor recognised, in the Comunn Eachdraidh collection, a photograph that his mother had in the house in Australia!

If your people left the Islands after 1850, then it should still be reasonably possible to trace them. The Census records for Scotland begin in 1841, and are available to the public up to 1891. The central repository is in General Register House in Edinburgh, but copies on microfilm are available in the Public Library in Stornoway. If you can find your family there, it will give the members of the family,

68

ages, and parishes of birth, and by working back through the census returns to 1841, you can build up a picture of the whole family, to be extended by local research in the village. Another source of fairly recent information is the Register of Births, Deaths and Marriages which starts in 1855. If you have, say, the date of a marriage in the Islands, one of the local Registrars will usually be happy to look it up for you in the Register, and let you have a copy of the Register entry. But two words of caution – dates are often only approximate, both in the Registers and in people's memories, so be prepared to search around the date you had in mind. And please remember that Registrars have a job to do also, and don't expect them to drop everything to assist you – they can hardly keep a prospective bride and groom waiting while they search with you! Registers for Stornoway, Barvas and Lochs parishes are held by the Registrar in Stornoway, and those for Uig, Carloway, Harris, North Uist, Benbecula, South Uist and Barra are available from the local registrars in these areas.

For the period before 1851, there are still some sources, but neither so many nor so complete as for later dates. The Old Parish Registers of the Church of Scotland contain Marriage and Baptismal Lists for most of Lewis. In Barvas and Stornoway parishes, these start in about 1810, and are fairly comprehensive up to the time of the Disruption in 1843, and the setting up of the Free Church. In Lochs and Uig parishes, the Registers do not start until the 1820s, and they are much less complete. Indeed in the Shawbost area, which at that time formed part of Lochs parish, the records are almost non-existent.

In Harris, Registers start in 1827, but after the first few years, only the farmers, merchants etc. are to be found there. In North Uist, the Register covers only the Kilmuir Church area, from Bayhead to Griminish, and if there were registers kept for Carinish and Trumisgarry areas, they have not been preserved. In South Uist and Barra, there are Church of Scotland Parish Registers also, but of course there are only a very few entries. The originals are again held in Register House in Edinburgh, but microfilms are available in Stornoway Library.

In South Uist and Barra, however, there are the Roman Catholic Church records. In South Uist, which included Benbecula, there are registers for Ardkenneth and Bornish which start in the 1820s and run to after 1855. The registers for Ardkenneth in the 1840s and 1850s are particularly valuable, as they frequently give patronymics in addition to English names. As an example, there is a baptism in Torlum, Benbecula, of a son to John MacMillan, or John of Angus of Donald of Malcolm – you can imagine what a prize that would be to a family tracer! In Barra, the registers start even earlier, in 1805, but there are several gaps of a year or so. These Registers are usually available from the local priests, in addition to New Register House in

Edinburgh. A word of caution, however, about these various registers. It has to be remembered first that there is a great duplication of names in the Islands, and also that many occurrences were never recorded in the early registers. So, although you may have found an entry with the names you are looking for, bear in mind that there could well be other families with the same names.

So always check later records also, in case the family you have found continues to appear in the census etc. after the date when your people emigrated. And remember also, that, particularly in the early Civil Registers, much of the information came to the Registrars at second hand, and may or may not be wholly accurate. Church records also have to be treated with caution, as, for example, the register of a baptism may not state the age of the person baptised, and the assumption of a very young child may not always be correct.

If your ancestor left the Islands before 1830, then you do have a problem! Much of the emigration then was to Cape Breton or elsewhere in Nova Scotia. Neither Scotland nor Canada was keeping accurate registers then, and many of the emigrants went across unofficially, and do not appear in the official lists of boats and passengers. To have any chance of success at all, you would have to have fairly accurate information from the Canadian side, such as the date of emigration, and a reference to the family in the earliest available Canadian census. Even with this as a starting point, tracing a family at that distance is usually a job for the specialist. There are several professional genealogists working in Edinburgh, but a recent development has been the opening of a local Genealogy Centre for the whole of the Western Isles.

This Resource Centre is at present located in the old schoolhouse in Northton, Isle of Harris. Most of the written sources mentioned are available there, along with many estate papers, and the proprietor's own extensive library of family tree files. A professional genealogical research service is available, covering the whole of The Western Isles, and many researchers, especially into early emigrants, have found that prior consultation has made it possible to do much of the preparatory work prior to coming to the Islands.

This does have the advantage of getting a lot of the basic paperwork out of the way while people are still at home and have access to supplementary information. So often people come here hoping to trace their ancestors, and have to leave without doing so, because they did not have with them information which would have been readily available at home, had they only thought to research it before coming to the Islands. And to someone who has saved up for years for the fare, it must be doubly galling to be successful in tracing the family only after the long awaited visit is past.

So my advice to any family seeker would be to do your homework before you come, to consult all the available sources before you leave home, in the hope that once you arrive here, you will be able to link into the locally available information. I can still recollect the sight of an old lady from Canada, who had been able to find the site of her great-grandparents' house, to meet third cousins, but above all, to look around and see all the stories she had heard from her grandmother taking form around her.

To see places, to meet people, to understand the past – surely these are the delights of successful family tracing?

ANGLING

Game Fishing

The Western Isles offer the visitor almost unlimited opportunities for brown trout fishing. Salmon and sea trout lochs are privately owned, but permission can be given on some estates in exchange for a fee (early application is advised). There are no coarse fish. Rivers are few and almost all are privately owned, but loch fishing is widely available. Brown trout fishing is also privately owned but can either be had free by permission from an estate for a modest fee, or by temporary membership of some angling associations. Outside the estates, boats are not easily available making bank fishing the most common method.

Fly fishing is the rule on estate salmon waters and on those controlled by angling associations. Worm or spinner can often be used elsewhere waters, but check very carefully that it is allowed before you begin fishing. Visiting anglers will find that their normal single-handed trout rods will be sufficient for all game fishing – even for salmon which, for the most part being summer fish, average around 6 pounds. Even the bigger ones (and there are some) can be dealt with on light tackle because lochs are usually snag free. Rods of 10 feet or longer are common in boat fishing, but don't feel constrained to any length that does not suit you.

The following selection of flies in sizes 12 and 8 will work for trout, sea trout and salmon, but by all means bring your own special favourites. These, however, will give you a reliable basis to work from:

Black Pennell, Butcher, Black Zulu, Blue Zulu, Invicta, Gruise (or Mallard) and Claret, Peter Ross and Soldier Palmer.

Some 14s for calmer waters and 6s for a big blow can be useful. Nylon monofilament for casts can be from 3 to 10 lbs. Most trout fishing is done with 5 or 6 lbs nylon and sea trout/salmon with 8 or 10 lbs, but do not feel restricted to those breaking strains.

For a day on the moor have good waterproof clothing, a stout pair of gumboots (waders are unnecessary), and carry enough food and drink for an energetic day. The relevant Ordnance Survey maps and a compass will be found useful in locating lochs – and just might become essential if you stay out too long and need help in getting back to your car. The freedom of a day's trouting, moving from loch to loch, is something to be experienced and treasured. Although The Western Isles have only 1% of the UK land area, they possess 16% of its fresh water area. You will not run out of lochs. In many parts of The Western Isles Sunday is respected as the Sabbath. Please observe

Freshwater loch near Uig, Lewis

local feeling and do not fish on that day. It is also against the law of the land to fish during the weekly close time.

Two very useful books on trout fishing are: *Trout Fishing in Lewis* by Norman MacLeod and *70 Lochs, A Guide to Trout Fishing in South Uist* by John Kennedy.

When planning salmon and sea trout fishing, the earliest contact should always be made with those estates offering such fishing. Advertisements can be found in the angling press.

Sea Angling

To the visiting sea angler, The Western Isles offer a variety of sport unsurpassed almost anywhere else in the country. There are excellent pollack and saithe in the tide races around the numerous rocky headlands; haddock and whiting over a wide variety of sea-bed conditions; cod and ling around the underwater reefs; and excellent thornbacks and flatties in the mud and sand, often in shallow inshore conditions. Add to this the rod bending excitement of a fight with the tenacious conger and skate, or the humble (but delicious) mackerel, caught on a hand line by the family, and there is something for everyone.

Traigh Seilibost, Harris

The specimen hunter will find much to excite him in this area, as the records of local sea angling groups will verify. If the visitor wishes to explore on his own he will certainly find fish, but there is no substitute for the expertise of the local fisherman, and local anglers will always share their experience. Tackle and techniques in these islands tend to be traditional, and a three-hook paternoster simply fashioned from heavy monofilament, with a lead at the bottom, meets most needs. Bait is freely available with innumerable beaches, muddy flats and tidal rocks for the keen bait hunter.

Organised competitive sea angling is centred on Stornoway, Lewis, Tarbert, Harris and Benbecula. There are two excellent Boat Festivals offering magnificent prizes, which usually take place in consecutive weeks in July/August. The Western Isles Open Boat Championships, centred in Stornoway, is considered to be one of the foremost events on the Scottish circuit in terms of organisation, fishing sport and entertainment, and more recently the Uist Open Boat Championships has proved to be a well run and popular event.

Hebridean Dishes

The nature of the land, the use of the sea as a food source and the isolation of the islands are the main factors deciding the diet of the Hebridean. Simplicity of preparation and cooking are the main characteristics of the island approach.

Fried herring with oatmeal

Clean, dry and trim the herring, score across the skin slantwise in two or three places on each side. Sprinkle with pepper and salt and toss in coarse oatmeal on a sheet of kitchen paper until thoroughly coated. An ounce of oatmeal and the same quantity of oil or fat should be allowed for every two herrings. Lightly fry until browned.

Poached Salmon (Bradan Slaopach)

Take one salmon freshly caught, water, lemon juice, salt, pepper.
Place salmon steaks in a pan, cover with water and add salt, pepper and lemon juice. Simmer very gently for 15 – 20 minutes. Drain fish, remove skin, serve hot or cold.

Mackerel in brown sugar

Use only fresh fish. Fillet and place fish, brown sugar, salt in alternative layers in a dish and leave overnight. Next day wash the fish in cold water and poach in equal parts of vinegar and water for 5 – 8 minutes until cooked. Leave to cool and serve with salad.
Mackerel can also be cooked in the same way as herrings in oatmeal.

Fish head liver and oatmeal (Ceann Cropaig)

Mix fish livers in a bowl with sufficient oatmeal to make a moist paste, season with salt, pepper and sugar. Fill fish head with paste, simmer in a pan for 30 – 35 minutes. Remove filling from head plus surplus meat from the fish, eat hot or cold with boiled potatoes.

Cormorant (Sgarbh)

This is now a protected species, so this recipe is included for interest only.
Pluck the bird and singe with a hot iron or open flame. Boil for 1 – 2 hours until tender, eat hot with potatoes and vegetables. A soup can be made from the stock using: ½ cup oatmeal, ½ cup barley, chopped onion, salt and pepper to taste.

Skate wings

This fish is delicious fried in butter and a little vinegar. Some say it should be hung for 2 – 3 days to allow the sticky oil it contains to drain away – in parts of Lewis it used to be put on the dung heap for a few days.

Clean and scrape the wings, and plunge them into the boiling salted water for 3 – 4 minutes, then drain and leave to cool. Remove the skin and fry for a few minutes in butter, add 3 – 4 drops of lemon juice and serve with boiled potatoes.

Cockles (Scuibain/Coilleagan)

Rinse the shellfish in fresh water and boil for 3 – 4 minutes, strain and remove flesh from the shell. Fry for 2 – 3 minutes in a little butter, salt and pepper to taste.

Cockles are collected, using rakes, from Traigh Mhor, Barra (where the aeroplanes land).

Salt herring

Salting – A traditional method of preserving food.

Clean and lay the fish alternatively with a good layer of coarse salt, ideally in a strong wooden barrel.

To Cook – Wash the herring to remove the salt, boil for 8 – 10 minutes until cooked and eat with boiled potatoes.

Cod, Conger, Mackerel and other fish can also be salted.

Brose (Brothas)

O gie my luv Brose, Brose
O gie my luv Brose and Butter
    Robert Burns (Gie my luv Brose)

Pour two handfuls of oatmeal into a bowl, add salt and a piece of butter, pour in boiling water to cover the oatmeal and stir it up roughly with a spoon, eat with sweet milk.

Black Pudding (Maragan Dubha)

Clean and wash one sheep's stomach inside and out.

Mix in a bowl 8 oz suet, 2 chopped onions, 8 oz oatmeal, 1 pt sheep's or pig's blood. Place in stomach bag, sew ends and boil gently for 2½ hours. Prick bags to prevent bursting.

For white pudding (Maragan Geala) make as above without the blood and double the quantity of oatmeal.

When cooked allow to cool – cut into slices and fry or grill.

Sheep's Head Broth (Brot Ceann – Caorach)

Sheep's head, barley, carrot, turnip, onion, parsley, cabbage, salt and pepper.

Prepare the head the day before cooking. Using a red hot poker, rub over the sheep's head until a nice brown colour, remove ears, horns and burn off any remaining wool. Split the head longways with an axe or saw. Remove brains and rub them well into skin of head. Put the head into a bowl of cold water with a handful of washing soda

Early kitchen utensils

and soak overnight. Wash well in clean water, place in a pan of boiling salted water and cook for 1½ hrs. Add the barley which has been soaking and all the vegetables chopped. Boil for a further 1½ hrs, remove remains of skull and serve hot.

Boiled Mutton
Place a 3 – 4 lb piece of leg or shoulder of mutton in a pan of boiling salted water, skim after 5 mins then simmer while preparing vegetables, carrots, turnip, onion and barley. Cut into small even pieces and add to the meat, and cook 20 minutes per lb plus 20 minutes. Serve with boiled potatoes.

Crowdie (Gruth)
Let a gallon of milk from the cow stand until thick and sour. Place in a pan and heat slowly until a curd is formed. Strain in a muslin bag or colander until dry (2 – 3 hrs). Add enough double cream to flavour the cheese and mix in thoroughly. Serve with hot oven scones.

Young gannet (Guga)
Wash the bird in cold water and soda, place into a pan of cold water and bring to the boil. Then skin and cook for a further 1 – 2 hrs. Change the water 2 – 3 times during cooking. Remove from the pan when cooked and cut into portions. Serve with boiled potatoes.

A GEOLOGICAL INTRODUCTION

Supposing we were able to take a giant knife and slice into the skin of the Earth to see what lies below it – what would we find? Try to imagine an apple as a model of the Earth. The skin of the apple is roughly equal to the depth of the Earth's crust, which varies between 10 and 35 km thick. Immediately under the skin of the apple, near the base of the Earth's crust, in a region corresponding to the root zone of a mountain range on the scale of the present day Himalaya, we would find rocks similar to those which we see in The Western Isles today. Geologists call this rock type 'Lewisian gneiss', and define it as a metamorphic rock. This means that Lewisian gneiss was once a variety of different types of rock, perhaps volcanic lavas, or granite, sedimentary mudstones or sandstones, all of which were then subjected to intense temperatures and pressures within the Earth. The resulting rock appears totally different from its original parent material and is called a gneiss.

For rocks which have been formed so deep within the Earth to be found at the surface today naturally involves the removal of an enormous quantity of material – and this of course requires a long time-span to accomplish. To anyone who becomes interested in these old rocks of north-west Europe, perhaps the first impression is their enormous age. It is central to the understanding of Precambrian rocks (rocks formed before 570 million years ago [m.y.a]) because this long history makes it difficult to separate individual geological events with the usual degree of scientific accuracy. Each period of intense heat and pressure changes the rocks to a different form, and more or less destroys all pre-existing structures, so that in complex areas only the age of the last event may be preserved.

To try to put the time-scale into perspective, if we could compress the whole of geological time, (from the formation of the Earth around 4,600 million years ago to the present day) into one year, then the time-span of one million years would pass in two hours. On this time-scale the volcanic rocks of Skye, Rum, and St Kilda would have formed about the beginning of the last week of December and North Sea oil would have formed about the second week of December. The Cairngorms, Ben Nevis and many of the Highland mountains had developed around the middle of November, by which time the Lewisian rocks of the north-west of Scotland were already very old. Although the Precambrian era would end around the last week of October, the rocks of the Outer Isles were formed from early February (2,900 m.y.a) until the middle of June (1,500 m.y.a.) when they would have looked much the same as at present although still deeply buried.

Much of The Western Isles was already formed before 2,900 m.y.a. and this type of gneiss has been through so many changes that it is very difficult to say with any certainty what the original rock-type was. As a result it is simply called 'grey gneiss' because of its appearance. It is the most common rock-type in The Western Isles, forming most of Lewis and North Harris and much of the Uists and Barra, so it is the rock which you will most commonly see as you travel through the islands. As the actions of wind and weather set to work eroding the old land surface, gradually deeper and deeper levels of the crust became exposed at the surface. The solid rock which was worn down was steadily removed and deposited as sands and muds on the surface of the Earth – in exactly the same way as is happening at present. Later, the combined heat and pressure connected with large scale earth movements in the crust changed these sediments to form meta-sedimentary gneisses. These rocks are found in Lewis at the tip of Ness, along the south coast of Harris, in roadside outcrops around Borve in Harris, and in a broad belt from Lochmaddy to Baleshare in North Uist, as well as other scattered localities. These meta-sediments are easily recognisable because of their flaggy appearance and earthy brown colour of weathering, which is usually set off by thousands of glittering silvery scales of the mineral called mica.

Standing at the Butt of Lewis lighthouse, or at the harbour at Port of Ness, it is easy to think of the flat lying rocks which you can see there as blankets of sediment covering the basement rocks. This is especially true at Port of Ness, where a modern equivalent is available for comparison in the cliffs of banded sands and gravels which run along behind the beach.

Later, the Lewisian complex was further added to by the rocks of South Harris which are the root an an ancient volcano. Collectively these rocks are often considered the stars of Hebridean geology. The rock-types are varied and exotic, but they have at least one common bond – they were all forced into position as molten rock which then cooled and solidified very, very slowly. First to be squeezed into place was a rock type called anorthosite, consisting mostly of a whitish mineral called feldspar. Anorthosite is important for at least two reasons, firstly it is only found in large quantities in the old, Precambrian areas of the Earth, notably in Greenland, Canada, and northern Russia. Secondly, as no significant mineral deposits occur commercially within the islands, anorthosite is one of the few rock-types which has any economic potential.

The anorthosite was followed by the emplacement of a mass of gabbro – the same type of rock which forms the Cuillin of Skye, though of course it doesn't look the same because it has been altered by subsequent heat and pressure. Most exposures of this rock, known as meta-gabbro are not directly by the roadside, but if you are interested it is well worth the short walk off the road to see this lovely rock. Large, dark red, circular garnets, some the size of a 10p piece, are crowded throughout the meta-gabbro, which otherwise consist of dark crystals of amphibole, and wispy white trails of quartz. The meta-gabbro stretches south-east in a narrow band from the Northton area, passing north of Roneval, to come out on the east coast to the north of the Lingerbay area. It forms the southern flank of the next member of the complex. The tonalite was emplaced next in the history of this part of Harris. This is a rock type similar to granite which formed a wedge-shaped mass, widest in the west and tapering eastwards towards Finsbay. Perhaps the best place to get a view of the tonalite is on the coast between Bagh Steinigie and Sgeir Liath on the west coast. As a general rule, when studying the geology of the islands it is far better to stick to coastal exposures and road cuttings rather than set off tramping around the interior. Much of the flat-lying land is thickly covered by peat bogs and by glacial material deposited after the last ice-age, which covers the solid rock from sight.

In the formation of the gneisses one of the last important events was the production of a vast amount of granite. This occurred around 18,000 m.y.a. to 15,000 m.y.a. and is commonly called Laxfordian Granite to distinguish it from other granites in different parts of the country. Most of the hilly areas of Uig and North Harris are formed of this Laxfordian granite, which is characteristically pink and white (from the feldspar and quartz), with shiny black (biotite) or silvery (muscovite) flakes, and dark, angular (amphibole) crystals. It is very easy to grasp that the granite must have been injected in liquid form into the surrounding rocks as it can clearly be seen to flow through earlier rock structures. A good place to observe this is in the roadside quarry beside the sheep-grid at Dalbeg on the west coast of Lewis. Alternatively, on the drive south from Tarbert, a very interesting change can be seen in the rocks. Around the Tarbert area and slightly south of this, the rocks are the basement grey-gneiss type. As you travel further south, stop at the quarry at Horsacleit. Here the first veins of granite are stabbing their thin white fingers into the older grey gneisses. You will see these veins becoming more common as you drive further south until in the roadside cuttings around Seilebost and Horgabost scarcely a square metre is unveined. In this area too the granite becomes so common that it forms large, pinkish, tilted sheets, sometimes several metres thick. Patches of granite become more frequent until suddenly, around Borve, the rock-type changes dramatically into the fine-grained, dark grey tonalites.

The final fling in the sequence is the injection of a very recognisable pink rock called pegmatite. These pink bands consist almost wholly of feldspar, quartz (white) and frequently silvery muscovite. You can see small patches of this throughout the islands and they are instantly noticeable because they contrast so markedly with the duller grey surrounding gneisses. Perhaps the easiest place to see this pegmatite is on the hill of Chaipaval to the north-west of Northton. If you have the time and the energy it would repay you to walk across this hill as it has a nice range of rock types in a small area. Leave the car at Northton and walk across the salt-marsh and machair to the northern end of the pink band. At its base you will find where it has been quarried and you may find some good samples of silvery muscovite on the spoil tips. The north-eastern edge of the peninsula is made up of the grey tonalites, and as you walk up to the top of Chaipaval you pass through an area of meta-gabbro where nice garnets are found, into the brown meta-sediments. These form the summit of the hill, and if you walk due south downhill the meta-sediments are replaced by more metamorphosed igneous rocks and meta-limestone on the south-west coast. The pegmatite band cuts through all of these rocks and therefore must obviously be the youngest rock type.

There must have been a great many dramatic changes in the crust of the Earth over the next 15,000 million years, but little evidence of this is shown in the islands today. Like a giant piece of sandpaper the surface of the Earth has been steadily worn down over the centuries, removing the younger rocks which had been laid down on top of the basement Lewisian gneiss. As a result, few of these younger rocks remain. The most significant of these is a small patch of sandstones around the Stornoway district which are between 280-200 million years old – comparative youngsters! These reddish rocks were trapped in a steep sided valley and so almost accidentally preserved from erosion.

So that in a nutshell is the geology of The Western Isles. As a slice of Earth history they are an isolated raft of stable, ancient basement surrounded by a variety of younger rocks. As a relict of the past they contain the first few, vaguely written chapters of the formation of our planet. As a stamping ground for a modern day geologist their subtle complexity is slowly being revealed, and with each tantalising discovery we begin to realise how much we really have still to learn from the rocks.

CLIMATE

The climate of The Outer Hebrides is dominated by two factors: the North Atlantic Drift, an oceanic current which brings a large body of relatively warm water into these northerly latitudes from the Gulf Stream, countering the Arctic influence; and the prevailing south westerly winds, mild but laden with moisture.

The following graphs and notes will help you to form a general impression of what to expect, although you should remember that these averages do not convey how rapidly conditions can change in the islands, or the possible variations of the weather on any given day within The Western Isles. Strong winds on an exposed beach on the west will be hardly noticed by those exploring a sheltered sea loch, beneath cliffs, on the eastern side. All data given is for Stornoway.

Average daily temperature

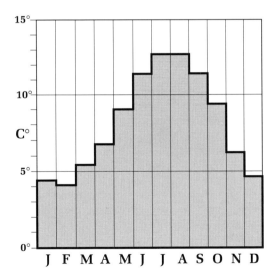

Highest temperature recorded: 25° on 30 July 1948

Lowest temperature recorded: -12° on 20 January 1960

Average monthly rainfall

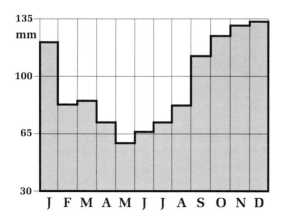

Maximum rainfall recorded in a 24 hour period: 57.5 mm on
18 January 1959

Average number of days with rain
(more than 0.2 mm)

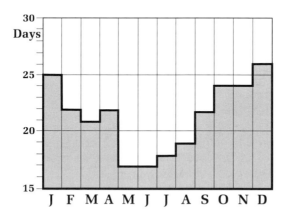

Wind direction

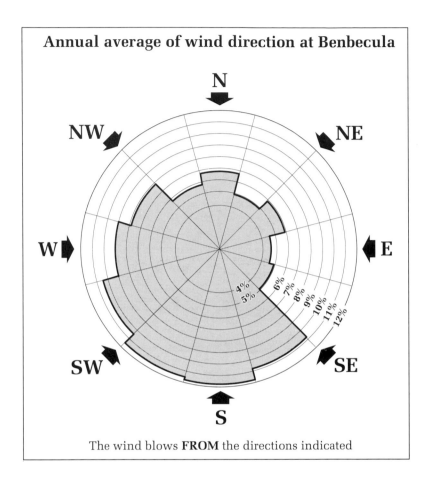

Annual average of wind direction at Benbecula

The wind blows **FROM** the directions indicated

The inherent mildness of the climate quickly disperses lying snow, which may be seen for up to 3 days in November, 8 days in December, 12 days in January, 7 days in February and 10 days in March. Records suggest you are most likely to hear thunder between October and February, and hardly ever in April. Fog and frost are minor features. Leaving aside the wind, which blows on two of every three days, it is a climate without extremes.

Wind speed

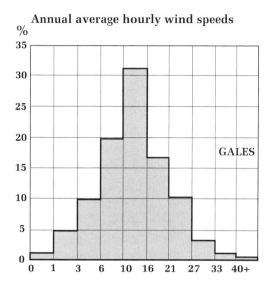

Days with gales

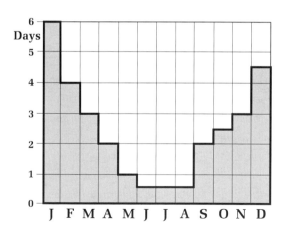

Maximum mean wind speed recorded: 54 knots on 28 September 1969

Maximum gust recorded: 98 knots on 12 February 1962

BIRDS OF THE OUTER HEBRIDES

The visitor arriving by air from Inverness or Glasgow or by road from Harris is inevitably impressed by the lack of trees until he reaches Stornoway. Here, occupying a magnificent setting by the sea loch and harbour, are the Stornoway Woods, or, as they are known locally, the Castle Grounds. These were planted by Mr & Mrs James Matheson (as they then were) in the mid 19thC century shortly after their purchase of Lewis and the building of the present castle. Many species of birds breed here and some, like the Treecreeper (*Certhia familiaris*), Blue and Great Tits (*Parus caeruleus: P. major*) and Mealy Redpolls (*Carduelis flammea*), are found nowhere else in the islands, except as vagrants. Warblers, such as Willow (*Phylloscopus trochilus*), Chiffchaff (*P. collybita*), Garden (*Sylvia borin*), Wood (*P. sibilatrix*) and Grasshopper (*Locustella naevia*) regularly turn up from year to year. A wandering Hobby (*Falco subbuteo*) and Great Spotted Woodpeckers (*Dendrocopos major*) are among the more exotic visitors, but there must be many more which escape detection in such an extensive area. The Woods hold the only rookery (*Corvus frugilegus*) and one of the few tree colonies of Herons (*Ardea cinerea*) in the islands.

Smaller groups of conifers and sycamores (*Acer pseudoplatanus*) in Glen Tolsta, Balallan, Valtos, Grimersta, Kinlochroag, Gisla and Eishken in Lewis, Rodel in Harris, on the slopes of Ben Aulasary and Ben Langass and at Clachan in North Uist, Loch Druidibeg, Allt Volagir, Grogarry in South Uist and Northbay and Brevig in Barra, provide shelter for vagrants and nesting Goldcrests (*Regulus regulus*), Collared Doves (*Streptopelia decaocto*), Starlings (*Sturnus vulgaris*) etc. Two large Forestry Commission plantations at Garynahine in Lewis and Aline in Harris are still young enough to hold interesting collections of birdlife and have been stocked with the only Pheasants (*Phasianus colchicus*) to be found in The Outer Hebrides. Many lochs and inland cliffs throughout the islands have sufficient rem-

nant cover of bushes and native trees, thus protected from fire and the omnipresent sheep, to harbour small birds and many Ravens (*Corvus corax*) and Hooded Crows (*C. corone cornix*), Red Grouse (*Lagopus lagopus*), Golden Plover (*Pluvialis apricaria*), Meadow Pipit (*Anthus pratensis*), Wheatear (*Oenanthe oenanthe*) and Stonechat (*Saxicola torquata*) are the most numerous denizens of the surrounding moorland.

Golden Eagles (*Aquila chrysaetos*) inhabit the mountainous territory of Lewis, Harris and North and South Uist where, from adjacent main roads, they may easily be seen at all times of the year. Buzzards (*Buteo buteo*) and Merlin (*Falco columbarius*) hunt over the moorland generally and the former are often mistaken for eagles. It could be said that any eagle seen perched on a fence post is, in fact, a Buzzard. Peregrine Falcons (*F. peregrinus*) may also be encountered infrequently, going somewhere fast. A few Hen Harriers (*Circus cyaneus*), Short-eared Owls (*Asio flammeus*) and Kestrels (*F. tinnunculus*) may be found on the western parts of the Uists and Benbecula but are absent from Lewis and Harris, except as strays. Long-eared Owls (*A. otus*) and Snowy Owls (*Nyctea scandiaca*) have occurred from time to time in suitable habitats. Ospreys (*Pandion haliaetus*) pass up and down the west coast in spring and autumn, pausing briefly at estuaries to fish. Other predators which have rarely been seen include White-tailed Sea Eagles (*Haliaetus albicilla*), Marsh Harriers (*C. aeruginosus*), Sparrowhawks (*Accipiter nisus*) and Gyrfalcons (*F. rusticolus*).

The main feature of the freshwater lochs of the Uists, Benbecula and Barra are Mute Swans (*Cygnus olor*) and Loch Bee in South Uist is remarkable for the hundreds which congregate on its shallow waters. This familiar bird is, however, absent from the lochs of Lewis and Harris, except as a vagrant, where, in winter, its place is taken by wintering Whooper Swans (*C. cygnus*) from Iceland. In summer, these lochs are home to Red- and Black-throated Divers (*Gavia stellata: G. artica*). The latter, amounting to about twenty pairs, are vulnerable to disturbance by anglers and boats and care should be taken to avoid their vicinity. But it is the shallow, machair lochs of the Uists and Benbecula which provide the birdwatcher with the greatest interest and an astonishing variety of ducks and waders. Shovelers (*Anas clypeata*) occur only here and share this habitat with Mallard (*A. platyrhyncos*), Teal (*A. crecca*), Scaup (*A. marila*), Shelduck (*Tadorna tadorna*), Wigeon (*A. penelope*), Gadwall (*A. strepera*), Garganey (*A. querquedula*), Pochard (*Aythya ferina*), Tufted Duck (*A. fuligula*), Coot (*Fulica atra*), Moorhen (*Gallinula chloropus*) and Little Grebe (*Tachybaptus ruficollis*). Rarer vagrants are occasionally found which have included a Bufflehead (*Bucephala albeola*), American Wigeon (*Anas americanus*), Green-winged and Blue-winged Teal (*A. crecca carolinensis: A discors*), Pintail (*A. acuta*) and a Pied-billed Grebe (*Podilymbus podiceps*). In Lewis Ring-necked Duck (*Aythya collaris*), a Red-crested Pochard (*Netta rufina*), Smew (*Mergus albellus*) and Goosanders (*M. merganser*) have been reported.

Off-shore, sea ducks occur in great numbers, especially, as already mentioned, in Broadbay in Lewis and the South of Taransay in Harris and in the sounds between the Uists and Benbecula and the south of Barra. Hundreds of Eider (*Somateria mollissima*) and Common Scoter (*Melanitta nigra*) gather in autumn in the Sound of Taransay, for example, and have been accompanied by Velvet and Surf Scoters (*M. fusca: M. perspicillata*), a King Eider (*S. spectabilis*) and Slavonian Grebes (*P. auritis*). These can be watched best from the dunes beyond the graveyard at Luskentyre. Great Northern Divers (*G. immer*) winter here as elsewhere. A Steller's Eider (*Polysticta stelleri*) spent more than ten years with the local common Eider at Peninerine in South Uist until 1983.

What most visitors come to the Hebrides to see are the seabirds. Apart from the common species like Herring (*Larus argentatus*), Great (*L. marinus*) and Lesser Black-backed (*L. fuscus*), Common (*L.*

canus) and Black-headed Gulls (*L. ridibundus*), which occur everywhere in large numbers, there are accessible colonies of Fulmar Petrels (*Fulmarus glacialis*) along the entire cliff-bound coastline and very occasionally inland. Kittiwakes (*Rissa tridactyla*) nest at Spainneavig at Ness, Swordale and Tiumpan Head in Lewis and on some of the uninhabited islands. Guillemots (*Uria aalge*)

A Fulmar Petrel

and Razorbills (*Alca torda*) nest at Spainneavig and on the headlands of the east coast of Lewis and elsewhere as in the case of the Fulmar. Black Guillemots (*Cepphus grylle*) are found commonly on all suitable cliffs. In winter arctic gulls, Iceland and Glaucous (*L. glaucoides: L. hyperboreus*), turn up, especially in Stornoway harbour, and in most years in considerable numbers. Of the rarer gulls there have been an Ivory (*Pagophila eburnea*) in Stornoway and in North Uist, a Mediterranean (*L. melanocephalus*) in Benbecula and a Franklin's (*L. pipixcan*) in South Uist. Sabine's (*L. sabini*), Little (*L. minutus*) and Ring-billed Gulls (*l. delawarensis*) are regular vagrants.

Common (*Sterna hirundo*), Arctic (*S. paradisaea*) and Little Terns (*S. albifrons*) breed near the aerodrome at Stornoway and elsewhere on the west coast as far south as Barra. Sandwich (*S. sandvicensis*), Black (*Chlidonias niger*) and Roseate Terns (*S. dougalli*) are not uncommon visitors on migration. One Gull-billed Tern (*Gelochelidon nilotica*) was reported from South Uist in 1987 and White-winged Black Terns (*C. leucopterus*) from Ness in Lewis and

Snipe

Borve in Benbecula in the sixties.

Both British species of skua breed in The Outer Hebrides and may most easily be watched from the B895 north of Gress in Lewis. Arctic Skuas (*Stercorarius parasiticus*) have, however, colonised North Uist, Benbecula and, perhaps now, South Uist where they have been seen in suitable territory. The Great Skua (*S. skua*), on the other hand, is confined to Lewis, North Rona, one of the Shiant Islands, Mingulay and Barra Head. An extraordinary feature of mid-May in North Uist is the passage of immense numbers of Pomarine (*S. pomarinus*) and Long-tailed Skuas (*S. longicaudus*) off Aird an Runair, given suitable weather. This headland is adjacent to the only RSPB Reserve in The Outer Hebrides at Balranald and one well worth a visit, especially in summer, when Corncrakes (*Crex crex*) are audibly and sometimes even visually present. Red-necked Phalaropes (*Phalaropus lobatus*) used to breed here but only single birds have been seen in recent years, from which it must be assumed that human pressure has been too much for this attractive wader, as it has in other parts of the Uists and Benbecula, whence it has all but disappeared. The fertile machair and lochs of this reserve, rich in suitable food, are typical of the west coast of these southern islands and harbour a unique variety and abundance of waders, including Lapwing (*Vanellus vanellus*), Dunlin (*Calidris alpina*), Ringed Plover (*Charadrius hiaticula*), Redshank (*Tringa totanus*), Oystercatcher (*Haematopus ostralegus*) and Snipe (*Gallinago gallinago*).

A National Nature Reserve at Loch Druidibeg in South Uist is nationally important for its coastal habitats of lochs, dunes and machair and contains also typical peat and croftland and scrub woodland. A large native flock of Greylag Geese (*Anser anser*) nest on the islands of Loch Druidibeg. Many others nest elsewhere in the Uists and Benbecula.

Although few visitors will manage to visit them, mention must be made of the many off-lying islands (most of which are now uninhabited) on account of their birdlife. Sula Sgeir, 40 miles north of the Butt of Lewis, has an important population of Gannets (*Sula bassana*) which have been harvested annually in August and September by the men of Ness since time immemorial. Neighbouring North Rona, the Shiant Isles in the Minch, the Flannan Isles west of Lewis, the Monach Isles west of the Uists and the islands south of Barra are all important refuges and breeding places for our birds and should be respected by visitors.

So many birds in The Outer Hebrides are living at the edge of their European sub-arctic boundaries that they are very vulnerable to disturbance; the Red-necked Phalarope has already been referred to in this context. All visitors should therefore be particularly careful not to intrude upon breeding birds and to do nothing to harm the place where they live.

Up to 1986 310 species of birds had occurred in the Outer Hebrides (excluding St Kilda). Of these nearly 200 turn up annually and about 100 breed regularly.

It is fair to say that few, if any, regions of Britain can produce such a variety of birdlife in such diverse surroundings.

References:
Peter Cunningham. *Birds of The Outer Hebrides*. Melven Press. Perth 1983.
Peter Cunningham. *A Hebridean Naturalist*. Acair. Stornoway. 1979.
Peter Cunningham. *The Castle Grounds*. Stornoway Gazette. 1979.

FLORA OF THE OUTER HEBRIDES

The Outer Hebrides is a marvellous place to see wild flowers. The visitor can relish the colours and the scents at their best among the west coast machair, with the calling of birds will adding another dimension to the experience.

It is the weather, however, which dominates all plant and animal life, with a preponderance of strong wind, mainly from the west. There is also a high frequency of rain and low cloud, although the islands do benefit from relatively mild winters and infrequent hard frosts. This cloud and rain has given rise to conditions which have created vast peatlands and wetlands, so much a feature of the central and eastern parts. Geology is another strong influence, with Lewisian gneiss, one of the oldest rocks in the world, giving acid soils and favouring only plants which can tolerate such conditions.

Over countless centuries, the prevailing westerly winds have blown large amounts of calcium rich shell sand over the western plains, enriching the land and creating the machair soils. In the same way lochs and lochans have also been enriched, and these support a rich flora, which in turn provides feeding for the swans, wildfowl and waders which breed or winter in The Outer Hebrides. The machair extends along much of the western coast but is seen at its best in the Uists, though it also occurs on Harris and Lewis. In high summer the machair is ablaze with colour, and most memorable on clear sunny days.

The coasts may be rocky and exposed, with countless offshore islets or stacks, or they may be more sheltered, with sand dunes or salt marshes. Many of the cliffs are clothed with the white-flowered Sea Campion, and where the salt spray splashes the rocks, the Sea Pearlwort. Sea Plantain may be seen on all of the coasts, along with the pink flowers of Sea Thrift. Less frequently there are the yellow flowers of the Kidney Vetch. A good place to see these plants is at Traigh Geiraha, north of Tolsta, where Scots Lovage also grows. Other very fine cliffs are at Mangersta, south-west of Uig. The dark green fern, Sea Spleenwort, grows in many coastal cliff recesses, and may even be seen inland at Glen Valtos, east of Uig Sands.

Sea Thrift

Common Scurvygrass is plentiful,

but look also for some less common flowers. There is plenty of Scottish Scurvygrass, but search for the rarer Danish Scurvygrass. The blue flowers of the Spring Squill may be found among cliffs on the west of Lewis, or on Barra, while some cliffs may have Early Purple Orchis on grassy ledges. Rock Sea Spurrey is a rarity found on low cliffs on the east of the Uists.

Salt marsh turfs are usually composed of Sea Thrift and Sea Plantain. When the Sea Thrift is in bloom during the early summer, the salt marshes can look like pink carpets against the blue sea. Perhaps the best place to see this is at Trumisgarry, North Uist, a few miles north-west from Lochmaddy. Other interesting salt marsh plants to seek out are the Saltmarsh Flat-sedge, the Baltic Rush and the rare Sea Rush. Of the spurreys, the Lesser and Greater Sea Spurreys are the most frequent, but Sand Spurrey is restricted to the Stornoway area.

Salt marsh pools may have the Beaked Tasselweed, at Luskentyre for example, in Harris, but the Spiral Tasselweed is a nationally rare species in North Uist. Eelgrass is commonly washed up with the tide from the extensive underwater 'meadows' which may on a calm day be seen from a boat. There are good salt marshes in Lewis at Coll, Gress and Tong all north of Stornoway, while in Harris there are fine examples at Northton and Luskentyre. In the Uists, some of the best may be seen at Newtonferry, Trumisgarry, Baleshare, Clachan and Howmore.

Sand dunes in The Outer Hebrides are often an outer fringe to the machair. Dunes, salt marsh and machair often merge into each other. The plants which grow in association with the dunes help to bind the mobile sand, and above the high water line greyish green sweeps of orache may give way to pink Sea Rocket, white-flowered Sea Sandwort, yellow Silverweed with silvery leaves, and pink Sea Milkwort. In this zone Sand Couch also grows, while other grasses binding the higher dunes are the abundant Marram and the less common Lyme-grass.

Among other interesting dune flowers are Whitlow Grass, Hoary Whitlow Grass, Hairy Rock-cress and Rue-leaved Saxifrage. Sand Sedge is abundant, but less common is the Curved Sedge, seen only in the north-west of Lewis and west Harris. Among the best sand dunes are those at Eoropie in the north of Lewis, Uig Sands in the west of Lewis and Coll, Gress and Traigh Mhor, Tolsta north of Stornoway. In Harris, there are fine dunes at Northton, Luskentyre and also at Hushinish, opposite Scarp. The island of Berneray, off North Uist, is accessible by ferry, and has excellent dunes and machair, while on the Uists themselves, there are good systems at Newton, Baleshare, Howmore, Askernish and Daliburgh. Barra has wonderful dunes at Eoligarry, Allasdale, Borve and Halaman Bay, and you can cross on a day trip to the dunes on Vatersay.

The machair colours speak for themselves, and on still summer days are enlivened by the singing of Skylarks and Meadow Pipits, calling Oyster Catcher and Redshank, drumming Snipe as well as other birds mentioned earlier. Much of the colour comes from the profusion of common wild flowers such as buttercups and clovers, Yellow Rattle, eyebrights and even Common Ragwort.

Orchids are a speciality of the machair, and the numbers are often astounding. The Hebridean Orchid, an endemic subspecies more or less confined to the Hebrides, is widespread and often quite abundant. The Frog Orchid with reddish brown flowers is also present, a good place to see it being the Northton machair in Harris. Widely distributed orchids include Early Marsh Orchid, with flesh coloured flowers; Early Purple Orchid, purple but occasionally sporting pink or even white flowers; and the Greater Twayblade, over a foot tall and with yellow green flowers and two broad oval opposite leaves clasping the stem about halfway. Much less common is the Fragrant Orchid, present only on Barra, and the Greater and Lesser Butterfly Orchids. A good place to see the latter is between Leverburgh and Strond in South Harris.

Two gentians occur on the machair, the Field Gentian with lilac flowers and the much less common Autumn Gentian which has dull purple flowers. Two tiny ferns are worth searching for, the Moonwort which is locally abundant and the Adder's Tongue. Both are overlooked, blending as they do with green vegetation. The machairs of Northton and Luskentyre, on Harris, are outstanding, but even Barvas on Lewis supports masses of orchids. The Eochar area of South Uist is fine, and a favourite is the machair on the west side of Berneray, with carpets of Sea Sandwort and Lesser Meadow-rue. Another gem is the dry machair at Eoligarry, Barra with acres of Primroses during early summer.

There are dry machairs and wet machairs, and each support its own particular wild flowers. On the wet machair, the scarce Brookweed may be found at the seaward edges, mainly in West Harris and the Uists. So also may Parsley and Hemlock Water Dropworts. There are commoner flowers like the Marsh Pennywort, and less common ones like Fool's Watercress and Lesser Marshwort. Also a host of common flowers including the yellow Marsh Marigold, pink Ragged Robin, white umbrellas of Wild Angelica and tall, stout heads of Yellow Flag.

Marsh Marigold

No one who has visited the islands can fail to have noticed the extent of open water, river and stream, loch and lochan, hill loch and machair loch, marsh and fen. Many of the plants of these habitats are submerged, the pondweeds for example, and are perhaps the province of the specialist. But round the edges of many lochs there are also a variety of colourful flowers, such as the White Water-lily, with large white flowers each with conspicuous yellow stamens. The leaves float in an arc surrounding the flowers. Very occasionally, for example in North Uist, you may see the Yellow Water-lily. All four species of bur-reed may be found, while the fringes of many lochs may have beds of Bottle-sedge, a few the rare Greater Tussock Sedge or the recently rediscovered White Sedge, near Locheport in North Uist.

Sedges and rushes grow on all the shores, but look also for the many reedbeds in places such as Loch Tuamister, near Shawbost, Lewis, and Loch an Eilean, at Griminish on North Uist. Bulrushes grow only on the west of Lewis, at Bragar. On loch side marshes, you will see the deep purple flowered Northern Marsh Orchid. Colourful flowers of the buttercup family include the Common, Ivy-leaved, Thread-leaved and Brackish Water-crowfoots, while the shores often have Lesser Spearwort or the scarce Celery-leaved Buttercup. Channels between machair lochs may have dense patches of Mare's-tail and Amphibious Bistort, for example on Berneray at the south end of Loch Bhruist.

There are wooded islands in many of the lochs. In an almost tree-less landscape, these are a relic of the woodland scrub which once clothed the terrain before man changed the scene. Trees include birch, willow and Rowan, while shrubs include roses, brambles and Honeysuckle. Margins of the islands may have the splendid Royal Fern. There are good wooded islands by the Pentland Road a few miles from Carloway, Lewis. On Harris, the Golden Road south of Tarbert gives views over several lochs with wooded islands, while in the Uists the many examples include the National Nature Reserve at Loch Druidibeg, South Uist.

In the absence of trees, plantations assume greater importance. Last century, Sir James and Lady Matheson commenced the planting of some twelve hectares of the Castle grounds in Stornoway, using imported soil. At least seventy species of conifers and broad-leaves grow, with an undergrowth of shrubs. The tree cover supports plant, bird and insect populations which would otherwise be absent. You can walk through these woods over a variety of tracks, enjoying woodland scenes of great beauty, with flowers such as Germander Speedwell or Bird's foot-trefoil. Stornoway Castle Woods have the only Walnut tree in the islands.

There are smaller plantations in south-west of Harris, and at Northbay, Barra, while new forests on Lewis will provide the wood-lands of the future. Even small shelter belts such as those at Balallan and Laxay on Lewis or at Clachan on North Uist, are important habi-tats for birds. Elsewhere, woodland plants survive in the absence of trees, including Wild Hyacinth, Holly, Wild Strawberry, Ivy and Bugle.

Moorland covers most of the islands, particularly the central and eastern parts. In sequence through the season, you will see the purple Bell Heather, the pink Cross-leaved Heath and purple Heather. Moorlands sport the Heath Spotted Orchid, often in profusion, and the small yellow flowers of Tormentil. There are white expanses of Hare's-tail and Common Cottongrasses, small purple, pink or even white flowers of Heath Milkwort and sticky, insectivorous leaves of the sundews. The star shaped pale green leaves of Common Butterwort send up small purple flowers, while late summer brings the bright yellow flowers of the Bog Asphodel. Botanists will wish to see oceanic peatland flowers such as Marsh St John's-wort, Great and Oblong-leaved Sundews, Bog Myrtle, Pale Butterwort, Lesser Skullcap and White beak-sedge. Hidden among the Heather may be the tiny orchid, Lesser Twayblade.

The more energetic may wish to climb hills and mountains, such as Ben Mhor and Hecla on South Uist or the hills of North Harris. Because they are not high summits, and because of the rocky terrain, these hills are not spectacular for their flora, but there are some fine views to be had on clear days. Characteristic upland flowers include Alpine Meadow-rue, Alpine Lady's-mantle and Mountain Sorrel. There are saxifrages such as Purple Saxifrage and Starry Saxifrage, ferns such as Beech Fern and Parsley Fern, and Dwarf Willow on exposed tops. Some mountain plants come downhill, even to sea level, in The Outer Hebrides, including Bearberry, Alpine Bistort, Mountain Sorrel, Dwarf Willow, Purple Saxifrage, Roseroot and Moss Campion.

Alpine Lady's-mantle

In a brief description such as this, only some of the wild flowers of the islands can be named. For the visitor, there are many more to be found. In the interests of conservation, examine the flowers, photograph them if you wish, but please do not pick them. This applies particularly to the rare plants and the orchids. As well as maps, you may wish to carry books such as Collins *Pocket Guide to Wild Flowers* or *The Wild Flower Key*, published by Warne. On the hills, use stout footwear; elsewhere wellington boots will make access more comfortable. With these items plus waterproofs, you will feel better prepared for the tough terrain and changeable climate of The Outer Hebrides.

FAUNA OF THE OUTER HEBRIDES

There is a well-known biological school of thought which suggests that the smaller an island is, and the further away it is from the mainland, the lower the number of species it will support. A related theory states that the smaller and more remote an island is, the greater the proportion of maritime species which will be present. While these theories have probably been over-applied, there is some truth in them: certainly many animal groups have fewer species in The Western Isles than on the adjacent mainland, and most habitats support fewer species. In spite of this, many parts of The Western Isles seem remarkably rich in all forms of wildlife, particularly in late spring and early summer, when the machair is at its peak.

When it comes to native mammals, The Western Isles are indeed poorly off. There are no badgers, foxes, squirrels, wild cats, bank voles or common shrews (all of which are present in Sutherland and Wester Ross) and the pine marten was lost about 100 years ago, having been persecuted to extinction.

Among small mammals, pygmy shrews, field mice, house mice and brown rats occur on all the main islands and on many of the smaller ones, while the black or 'ship' rat survives on the Shiants. Field mice often inhabit houses, while the house mouse often spends the summer in the open! The brown rat is a recent incomer to Britain, and did not reach The Western Isles till the 18thC. The first colonists may have come ashore from the wreckage of the King of Prussia which foundered off Lewis in 1768. While our brown rats are often black in colour (black rats are often brown in colour!) the ship rat is now believed to be extinct except on the Shiants, where there are no brown rats and the shore and the seabird colonies afford a plentiful supply of food. Black rats which came ashore from a wreck on North Rona in 1685 are thought to have wiped out the human population by bringing Plague, but it is more likely that the rats ate all their grain and the people starved to death. There are pipistrelle bats in the Stornoway area. Short-tailed voles are absent from Lewis and Harris but frequent in the Uists.

Introduced hedgehogs are now common in southern South Uist and in the Stornoway area, and are occasionally reported elsewhere. Rabbits, brown hares and mountain hares have all been introduced. The rabbit is now a serious threat to machair stability in many areas; the mountain hare is scarce, and the brown hare may be extinct.

The only native ground predator is the otter, which lives mainly on the coast, or close to it. Unfortunately there are large numbers of introduced or escaped ground predators: feral cats, ferret-polecats and feral mink are all thriving, to the detriment of poultry and ground-nesting birds. Mink are now abundant on Lewis and Harris, but only a few individuals of this voracious predator are known to have crossed the Sound of Harris, where they could cause immeasurable damage to the internationally important breeding bird populations.

Red deer occur in small numbers in Pairc, Uig and North Harris, and marauders are occasionally seen elsewhere on the island. There is also a herd in South Uist and small numbers in North Uist, as well as a small herd on Pabbay in the Sound of Harris. Feral goats once existed in the hills of Harris and Uig but they have been extinct for many years.

The origins of the terrestrial mammal fauna have long puzzled biologists. Only a very few species have the ability to colonise naturally – possibly only otter and even deer and pygmy shrews (the last having excellent powers of dispersal) but the majority of even our 'native' mammals are thought to have been introduced by man – either deliberately or accidentally.

There are no less than three subspecies of the field mouse in The Outer Hebrides – one on Hirta (St Kilda), another on Mingulay and Berneray, and the third on the other islands. There is also a Hebridean subspecies of the house mouse, and a second, the St Kilda house mouse, died out shortly after Hirta was evacuated in 1930.

These subspecies are thought to have evolved very quickly because so few of them were involved in the founding population. Analyses of the skeletal characteristics of the field mice of the Scottish islands suggests that they are more closely related to Scandinavian field mice than to those of the British mainland, and it is believed that they were accidentally imported by the Vikings.

The history of introductions, however, is an unhappy one. Virtually every deliberate introduction has become a pest. Even species which are regarded as beneficial on the mainland, such as the apparently innocent hedgehog, can become serious pests in island situations. Unfortunately it is perfectly legal to import species native to Britain, so that anyone importing a fox might be guilty of gross irresponsibility, but would not have broken the law. Even the importation of species which are already here could cause problems, by diluting or even wiping out island subspecies. The lesson is clear – no animals should be introduced without seeking expert advice – the consequences of well-meaning introductions could otherwise be disastrous.

Marine mammals are well represented. Some of the offshore islands of The Outer Hebrides support internationally important breeding colonies of grey seals, and the Monach Isles are now thought to form the second largest colony in the world. Other colonies include Shillay, Gasker, North Rona, and Haskeir. Common seals are probably less numerous, and are more difficult to count as they do not breed in large colonies and the pups can swim immediately after birth. Common seals tend to breed in sea lochs rather than on uninhabited islands, but both species may be seen in sea lochs. There are a few records of unusual seals, including harp and hooded seals, but the most spectacular wanderer must be the walrus, which has been seen on several occasions.

Whales and dolphins are more numerous in Hebridean seas than most people realise. The large whales are now uncommon world-wide, but The Western Isles once supported its own whaling industry based at Bunaveneader in West Loch Tarbert. The commonest whales in inshore waters are

Grey seal and pup

the minke and the pilot. The latter is sometimes involved in mass strandings and is still fairly numerous. Killer whales also occur, and recent records of unusual species include a beluga in Loch Roag. White-beaked dolphins are numerous in the northern Minch in summer, and there seems to be a resident population of Risso's dolphin in the same area. White-sided dolphins and porpoises may be seen throughout the islands. A boat is desirable if you wish to see whales and dolphins at their best, but they should never be chased. Any boat venturing north from Stornoway will usually pick up dolphins around Chicken Rock, and good sightings of dolphins and even minke whales may be obtained from the shore at Tiumpan Head and Portvoller Bay.

The only reptile native to The Western Isles is the slow worm (actually a legless lizard), which is often seen basking in summer. While there are traditional stories of snakes these have yet to be confirmed. There are no native amphibians, but large numbers of tadpoles are tipped into lochs every year; in spite of very similar habitat supporting frogs on the mainland the tadpoles almost never survive, and such introductions should be discontinued. There are a few reported sightings of adult frogs, which may be derived from introduced tadpoles, but they are more likely to have been introduced as adults, though a breeding population seems to have become established in Great Bernera. There is one population of newts – in the Uists, thought to have been introduced. The only other reptiles which occur in our islands are marine turtles, which turn up from time to time. A leathery turtle was recently landed at Port of Ness, having drowned after entangling itself in ropes, and it is hoped that a cast from this animal will eventually be on display locally.

There are only a few species of fresh-water fish: salmon, brown trout, sea trout, charr – on Lewis and North Uist, three-spined stickleback, ten-spined stickleback and eel. Eels and three-spined sticklebacks are the most widespread, and there are spine-deficient populations of the latter in the Uists. Marine species may occur in rivers and in the brackish (mixed fresh and sea water) lagoons and lochs of the Uists.

There are many thousands of different types of invertebrates – over 600 species of beetle, for example – so that only the briefest account can be given here. 367 species of lepidoptera have been recorded in The Western Isles, including 15 butterflies, though some of these are rare migrants. The commonest species are the green-veined white, common blue, small tortoiseshell and meadow brown. Large and small heaths, large white and red admiral are also likely to be seen, as are the small white and the dark green fritillary, but only in the Uists and Barra – neither has been recorded on Lewis or Harris. Moths are too numerous to cover, but a colourful day-flying species, the magpie moth, is very common on moorland, and is often mistaken for a butterfly.

Other insects likely to attract attention are the dragonflies, of which we have ten species. The damselflies are the most numerous but the most spectacular is the huge (and uncommon) gold-ringed dragonfly.

Over 500 flies have so far been recorded, but only the cleg and the midge are likely to attract attention. Midge larvae form an important food supply for fresh water fish. Eight bumblebees occur, including the famous *bombus jonellus hebridensis*, which is common on moorland and merits a mention if only because everyone else mentions it – probably rather fewer people have seen it than have written about it.

We only have about half the number of beetle species present on the northern mainland, but this may be due to the lack of habitat rather than to the 'island rules' – much of the gap may be attributed to the absence of woodland species. Only the larger or more colourful species such as the splendidly named sexton beetles, or ladybirds (relatively scarce in most years), attract much attention.

Eighty-six mollusc species have been recorded on land and in fresh water in The Western Isles, compared with 108 on the northern mainland. Again, only the larger species are likely to be noticed by the casual observer, including the ubiquitous large black slug. Snails abound on the machair (where shell sand supplies the only locally available calcium for shell growth), including the large common snail and the smaller pale yellow or chocolate-banded garden snail. Other very common machair species are the flat heath snail and the pointed snail. In spite of the lack of calcium in the acid lochs and rivers, the rare pearl mussel, with its huge shell up to 15cm long, manages to survive in a few river systems on Lewis and Harris. Only a very small percentage of shells contain pearls, and it should not be collected, because of its rarity.

We have already seen that The Western Isles have a number of subspecies. Another feature of the fauna worthy of mention is that it seems to contain rather a high proportion of melanic animals, which are rather darker than usual, though the phenomenon is not so extreme as it is in Shetland. There are melanic varieties of birds, mammals, butterflies, moths and bees. While this has been attributed to the wet climate, there is not really any satisfactory explanation.

As many of the ecosystems of The Western Isles seem to contain fewer species than their mainland counterparts, they are more delicately balanced. Thus any interference in the species composition through introduction, or alteration of any important physical factor such as the nutrient balance of a loch, could have serious consequences for wildlife. Some of the machair and freshwater habitats and the flora and fauna they support are of international importance, and they should not be unnecessarily disturbed. If there is one message which comes across clearly from a study of the fauna, it is that the introduction of an animal to a locality where it did not previously exist should not be contemplated without expert advice. Otherwise there could be serious consequences not only for wildlife, but also for Man, who has enough problems in these islands without having to cope with alien pests.

THE SEASHORE

If the terrestrial fauna of The Western Isles may seem impoverished to visitors, the marine life of these relatively unpolluted seas seems extremely rich and varied, as indeed it is. The rich variety of marine habitats, from the most exposed cliffs to the most sheltered inlets, and the existence of tidal rapids and saline lagoons, greatly enhance this variety.

Though the west coast is exposed to the full might of the Atlantic rollers, a huge kelp forest off the Uists absorbs some of the waves' energy, so that the west coast of the Uists is not quite so exposed as that of the west of Lewis. Very exposed coasts tend to support only a few species, and rocky shores tend to be dominated by barnacles rather than seaweeds.

Ironically, the most sheltered of shores also tend to be rather poor in species, as there is little lateral movement of water to ensure a supply of larvae, nutrients or food. Thus the inner parts of sea lochs usually have the same few seaweeds and animals. Though nearly 300 types of seaweeds (algae) have been recorded in The Outer Hebrides, almost all of the algal growth consists of only a few species. There is a standard sequence of algae, with channel wrack at the top, giving way to a narrow band of spiral wrack; neither of these has air bladders. Below these there is usually a very broad mixed band of the two species with air bladders: bladder wrack with paired bladders and knotted wrack with large, single air sacs. Knotted wrack is collected and dried at Keose, to be processed on the mainland to produce alginate, used widely in food and household goods. The lowest of the wracks is saw wrack, so called because of the serrated edge to the frond. At very low tides the kelps are exposed – common kelp with its limp stalk and below, and rarely exposed, the stiff kelp, which stands erect. It is the latter which provides the shelter for the Uists and which, when it was washed ashore there and elsewhere in the winter gales, was burned in the early 19thC. While the kelp boom lasted, landowners encouraged their tenants to increase in number, thus laying the foundations for clearances and emigration when the kelp market collapsed.

Other conspicuous seaweeds include thong weed, with its intriguing buttons at the base; enteromorpha, the bright green alga which is often associated with fresh water flowing onto the shore and is often bleached white by the sun; and lithophyllum, a beautiful purple or pink calcareous crust which coats the lower rocks; a related species living offshore produces spectacular branched growths which are often mistaken for coral. Moderately exposed shores often have the slimy laverbread on the upper shore and a bladderless form of bladder wrack below.

The most obvious animals on the shore are molluscs. The winkles display a similar zonation to the wracks, with the small winkle living in crevices on the upper shore, the very variable rough winkle below, giving way to the flat winkle in the bladder/knotted wrack zone, with the edible winkle on the lower shore. Similarly, the top shells have the flat top above, the grey top in the middle, and the colourful, conical painted top at the lowest levels. Everyone is familiar with the common limpet, but careful searching of the richer lower levels may reveal the delicate tortoiseshell limpet and its pale pink relative, the white tortoiseshell limpet. Blue-rayed limpets live on kelp. The common mussel may grow to a good size on sheltered shores, but usually

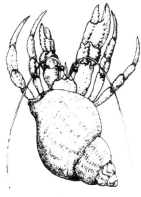

dies off in its first winter on exposed coasts. The much larger horse mussel occurs at lower levels. Barnacles and common mussels form the main food source for the common dog-whelk, the commonest rocky shore predator, easily distinguished from the winkles by the 'canal' at the base of the shell opening. Seemingly empty shells of this and other species are often inhabited by hermit crabs. The other very common predator is the shore crab, which has a serrated carapace – the edible crab has a 'pie-crust' edge. The most numerous anemone is the dark red beadlet anemone, but the very large dahlia anemone may be encountered on the lower shore.

Hermit crab

The richest rocky shores of all tend to be the tidal rapids, found where the large sea loch is connected to the sea by a narrow opening, as at Valasay in Great Bernera. Not only do 'lower shore' animals occur at higher levels, because of the constant flow of water, but many animals tend to be larger than normal, a phenomenon particularly noticeable in the sponges and starfish, especially the brightly coloured purple starfish. Here, too, one is most likely to come across the cup coral, like a sea anemone with a shell. Larger, colonial corals are occasionally dredged up on the edge of deep areas by fishing vessels. The commonest sea anemone in rapids seems to be the snakelocks anemone. Under low overhangs on rich shores one may be rewarded by the sight of a most appropriately named soft coral – dead man's fingers. At such low levels one may also encounter the common sea urchin or the smaller green sea urchin. Worms of many varieties are frequent on most rocky shores from the free living ragworms to the keelworms and coiled worms encased in calcareous tubes. Other animals likely to be found are the brittle stars and the fleshy sea squirts: neither should be handled. The commonest fish are the shanny and the butterfish.

Sediment shores support more life than might be supposed. Sand on the most exposed beaches is really too mobile to allow much fauna to take hold, but sandhoppers may be abundant around the strandline. Moderately exposed shores often have low densities of several types of worm, and swimmers may feel a slight tickling sensation on their legs – it is caused by eurydice, a small crustacean which loves surf – and, apparently, trying to nibble its way through human skin! It is, however, completely harmless. Swimmers need have no fear of the common jellyfish, a very numerous species with transparent flesh and purple rings, but should beware of all other types, which can sting even when lying 'dead' on the shore.

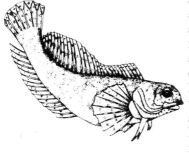

The shanny

Only the more sheltered beaches support molluscs, the commonest of which is the thin tellin, which may be white, pink, or even orange in colour. In Broad Bay and at Luskentyre the thin tellin may be joined by large numbers of the banded wedge shell, a larger species with a more solid, oval shell and beautiful concentric bands. Huge heaps of the empty shells of this species may be found from time to time on the Broad Bay beaches. Banded wedge shells seem to be more numerous on Lewis and Harris than anywhere else in Britain, but they are very scarce in the Uists. The siphons of tellins form an important source of food for young plaice which move inshore with the incoming tide. The only other fish likely to occur in the sand is the sandeel, which feeds on plankton.

Certain sheltered beaches may have sea potatoes, burrowing sea urchins which are often found minus their spines on nearby strandlines, and a few beaches have razor shells, which can be captured only by very agile or skilled people.

Estuaries are usually very sheltered, and they are often very rich in burrowing fauna. Indeed, close inspection of the surface of some estuarine muddy sand may reveal vast numbers of the spire snail, an important source of food for birds. The ragworms, horned shrimps, Baltic tellins and common cockles which occur in this habitat also provide an important source of food for birds. This food is particularly important in winter, when there may be large numbers of wintering birds and few alternative food sources.

Eelgrass, one of the few flowering plants to grow in the sea, occurs in a few estuaries, and uprooted plants may be found on strandlines on Harris and the Uists. Muddy shores occur at the heads of sea lochs: little is known about their fauna, but it is known to include ragworms and the peppery furrow shell.

The strandlines of beaches may yield almost anything which can float, and many objects which common sense suggests should not. No unidentified man-made object should be touched – it could be toxic or even explosive. Some idea of ocean currents may be gained from the fact that significant numbers of containers for the oil used by the North American Inuit (eskimos) for their skidoos have been found on our shores.

An immense range of seashells may be found on the strandline. The most interesting to the casual beachcomber are probably cowries (common and spotted varieties), the pelican's foot shell, necklace shells, smooth and prickly cockles, Faroe sunset shells, razor shells, the large oval otter shell, and the heavy, saucer-like Icelandic cyprina. The best beaches for shells are probably Scarista and Borvemore on Harris, and Traigh na Berie in Uig. Traigh Mhor in Tolsta yields large numbers of the beautiful thin lantern shell.

Stranded logs may contain lime-lined tubes created by the shipworm, actually a bivalve mollusc. Logs and plastic containers may have goose barnacles; these are so-called because barnacle geese were once thought to hatch from them.

People who wish to collect are encouraged to gather shells from the strandline rather than try to store shells captured alive – these rapidly develop a most offensive odour and are invariably discarded. It is quite possible to collect up to a hundred different shells from one beach if one is prepared to examine the minute shells of the strandline at close range.

When on the shore it is always essential to ensure that there is a return route if the tide comes in. The other golden rule is that boulders which are overturned must be replaced exactly as they were found – leaving boulders upturned kills the inhabitants, and is on a par with robbing the nests of scarce birds.

Snakelocks Sea Anemone

THE GUIDE SECTION

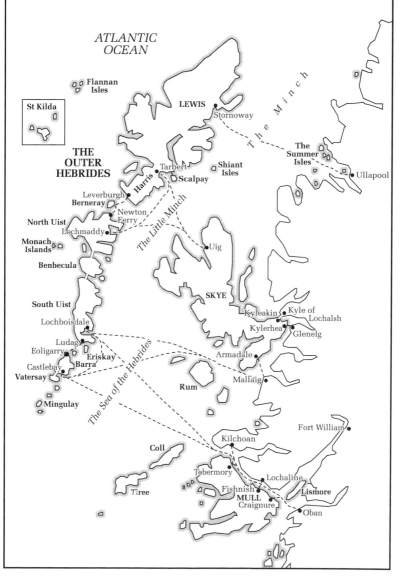

ATLANTIC
OCEAN

Flannan
Isles

St Kilda

LEWIS

Stornoway

The Minch

THE
OUTER
HEBRIDES

Tarbert

Harris

Scalpay

Shiant
Isles

The
Summer
Isles

Ullapool

Leverburgh
Berneray

Newton
Ferry

North Uist

Lochmaddy

The Little Minch

Monach
Islands

Benbecula

Uig

South Uist

SKYE

Lochboisdale

Kyleakin

Kyle of
Lochalsh

Kylerhea

Glenelg

Ludag

Eoligarry

Eriskay

Castlebay

Barra

Armadale

Vatersay

The Sea of the Hebrides

Mallaig

Rum

Mingulay

Fort William

Coll

Kilchoan

Tobermory

Lochaline

Fishnish

Lismore

Tiree

MULL

Craignure

Oban

105

EILEAN BHARRAIGH (BARRA)

Arrival and departure points

Bagh A Chaisteil (Castlebay) to Loch Baghasdail (Lochboisdale).
Caledonian MacBrayne. *2 hours.*
Bagh A Chaisteil (Castlebay) to Oban. Caledonian MacBrayne.
7 hours.
Eolaigearraidh (Eoligarry) to Eiriosgaigh (Eriskay) and Ludag, Uibhist
A Deas (South Uist). *Small passenger ferry.*
Bagh A Chaisteil (Castlebay) to Bhatarsaigh (Vatersay). *Causeway.*
Traigh Mhor Airport to Beinn Na Faoghla (Benbecula) and
Stornoway. British Airways.
Traigh Mhor Airport to Glasgow (via Tiree September to May).
British Airways.

Eilean Bharraigh (Barra), probably named after Saint Finnbarr, a Gaelic Scot who probably established a church at Eolaigearraidh (Eoligarry) in the early 7thC, is one of the most beautiful islands in The Outer Hebrides. It is about 8 miles long by 5 miles wide, and contains an extensive range of scenery from the craggy hills such as Heaval (384 m) with heather slopes to the broad grassy machair land and lovely silver beaches.

The main centre of the island is Bagh A Chaisteil (Castlebay), a large natural sheltered harbour which has shops, post office, bank, hotels, doctor and Tourist Information Centre. The new community school, a distinctive modern building at the edge of the village, has a library, and is the venue for many social and community events.

The centre of Bagh A Chaisteil (Castlebay) is dominated by Kisimul Castle, the ancient home of the Chief of the MacNeils (one of the oldest Scottish clans), built on a low, flat island which is almost covered at high tide. The present castle dates from the 15thC although it had been a stronghold for many centuries before that. It consists of a square tower with a curtain wall, within which there is a hall, chapel and other buildings. These surrounding walls used to have wooden galleries for defence, but they burned down in 1795. The legendary galley was berthed alongside on a sloping beach, with the crew-house nearby. The crew outside the castle were expected to defend it from attack, when it was used by all the people as a place of refuge. It had two artesian wells and a fish trap in a catchment basin. The castle was uninhabited and neglected from 1795 when the MacNeils stayed at Eoligarry House. In 1838 Eilean Bharraigh (Barra) was sold to Colonel Gordon of Cluny. A hundred years or so later the castle and much of the land was bought back for the MacNeils by

Robert Lister MacNeil, an American who became the 45th Chief of the Clan, and was at that time an architect. He supervised the restoration of the castle, and his son, the new Clan Chief, now uses it as a residence when on the island.

Overlooking Bagh A Chaisteil (Castlebay) is the handsome build-

Castlebay

ing of the Roman Catholic Church, Our Lady, Star of the Sea, representing a faith which has survived in strength from its introduction in the 6th-7thC.

At the beginning of this century Bagh A Chaisteil (Castlebay) was a thriving fishing port and the concrete platforms of the processing and curing stations can still be seen down by the shore. A more recent development is the new fish processing factory at Ardveenish, built by the Highlands and Islands Development Board and visited shortly afterwards by the Prince and Princess of Wales.

Across the bay is the island of Bhatarsaigh (Vatersay) with its lovely shell-sand beaches between two hills. On the west beach there is a monument in memory of the 'Annie Jane', an emigrant ship which was wrecked in 1853 with the loss of 450 lives, many of them islanders. On a rocky hill on Ben Oronsay is 'Dun a Chaolais', a circular broch about 9 m in diameter, but now in poor condition. On the island there are about five miles of roadway and it is well worth the trip across the new causeway, especially to enjoy the view of the smaller islands to the south – Sandray, Pabbay, Mingulay and Berneray.

On the west side of the island of Mingulay is the perpendicular face of the cliffs of Builacraig, which are 213 m high. Centuries ago the MacNeils, who owned the island, adopted the precipice as part of their crest and used the name as their rallying cry.

From Bagh A Chaisteil (Castlebay) there is a circular road of about 14 miles around Eilean Bharraigh (Barra). Heading west we pass between two hills, Heaval (384 m) to the east and Ben Tangaval (332 m) to the west. On the left-hand side is Loch St Clair, on which stands Castle St Clair or Dun Mhicleoid. This castle is about 5.4 m square and stands about 4.5 m high, and used to have three floors with an opening on the north side. Near the loch is a drinking well, marked by a white stone setting, and dedicated to St Columba. We see the Atlantic as we reach Tangasdale, where the new Isle of Barra Hotel overlooks a beach of silver sand.

Opposite the road which turns east to Borve there are standing stones in the field between the road and shore. The next turning is to the township of Baile Na Creige (Craigston), which leads by track to the centre of the island and by foot to Earsairidh (Earsary) on the east coast.

Beyond the road end you can walk to Dun Bharpa, a massive heap of tumbled stones surrounded by standing stones. This is a neolithic chambered cairn, probably used as a communal burial ground.

On the main road just past Allathasdal (Allasdale) overlooking the Atlantic, is Dun Cuier, an Iron Age fort with only the concentric foundation of stones left. Over grassy dunes to the west is Seal Bay where, on rocky ledges to the north, basking seals can be seen on fine days.

Before Bagh A Tuath (Northbay) is Loch an Duin, which has been dammed to provide the island's water supply. Near the loch are the ruins of the island's mill house. At the junction the road continues down the east coast back to Bagh A Chaisteil (Castlebay), passing Bruairnis (Bruernish), Earsairidh (Earsary) and the statue of the Madonna and Child erected by the islanders in 1954. The left fork of the road leads to Traigh Mhor and Eolaigearraidh (Eoligarry), while in Bagh A Tuath (Northbay) a statue of St Finnbarr can be seen holding a crook aloft. Traigh Mhor is a wide bay of shell-sand, used as the island's airport, but once famous for the wonderful cockles which even at the beginning of the 18thC provided one to two hundred cart loads each day of the spring tides. The cockleshell fragments are now gathered and processed for harling (a roughcast wall coating, common throughout Scotland) at the house built by Sir Compton MacKenzie.

As we approach Eolaigearraidh (Eoligarry) the road to the right leads to the small jetty which is the landing stage for the passenger ferry to Ludag on Uibhist A Deas (South Uist), and, on the left, Cille Bhara.

Cille Bhara in its present form was probably built around the 12thC, though there may have been some form of monastic cell there in the 7thC. The main church has two chapels on the east side. The north chapel or St Mary's Chapel has recently been re-roofed and houses the late medieval carved tombstones recovered from the graveyard. A copy of a runic stone is also on display, the original being housed in the National Museum of Antiquities in Edinburgh. The base of the altar can be seen at the east end of the main church, where the statue of St Finnbarr once stood. St Finnbarr's Feast Day is

Traigh Mhor Airport, Barra

still celebrated on the 27th September.

The walled remains of Eolaigearraidh (Eoligarry) House, where the MacNeil Chiefs built their home after leaving Kisimul Castle in 1790, is close by. The buildings were demolished in 1976 due to their dangerous condition. At Scurrival and further south there are some remains of Iron Age forts.

Our Lady, Star of the Sea, & The Craigard Hotel, Castlebay

UIBHIST A DEAS (SOUTH UIST)

Arrival and departure points

Loch Baghasdail (Lochboisdale) to Bagh A Chasteil, Eilean Bharraigh (Castlebay, Barra). Caledonian MacBrayne. *2 hours.*
Loch Baghasdail (Lochboisdale) to Oban. Caledonian MacBrayne. *7 hours.*
Ludag to Eiriosgaigh (Eriskay) and Eolaigearraidh, Eilean Bharraigh (Eoligarry, Barra). *Small passenger ferry.*

Uibhist A Deas (South Uist) is the second largest island in the Outer Hebrides, being some 21 miles long. The west coast is almost one long sandy beach with dunes and a mile or two of machair ground behind, which has allowed crofting and farming development. From the machair to the central mountainous spine the ground is rocky with peat and numerous fresh water lochs. The central mountainous area has two large peaks, Ben Mhor 620 m and Hecla 606 m, extending down to the rocky cliffs of the east coast. This coastline is broken up by four large sea lochs, Loch Baghasdail (Loch Boisdale), Loch Aineort (Loch Eynort), Loch Sgioport (Loch Skipport) and Loch A Charnain (Loch Carnan), which provide excellent natural harbours and are very popular anchorages for visiting yachts.

Loch Baghasdail (Lochboisdale) is the main sea port for the island. Those arriving by ferry should look out for the ruins of a 13thC castle on Calvay island, at the entrance to the loch. In Loch Baghasdail (Lochboisdale) you will find a hotel, police station, post office, medical and dental clinics, garages with taxi services, school, shops and Tourist Information Centre. The township is of fairly recent origin, and has a population of about 300, being populated after the clearance of the west side by Colonel Gordon of Cluny, who bought the island from Clanranald in 1838.

From Loch Baghasdail (Lochboisdale) the road heads west to the main north south road at Dalabrog (Daliburgh). The small community here has a hospital and eventide home run by the nuns of the Sacred Heart. There are also shops, a hotel, a school and a petrol station. Five miles south is the charming 19thC Pollachar Inn with fine views south to Eiriosgaigh (Eriskay). Close by are the standing stones from which Pol A Charra (Pollachar) takes its name. A few miles further on is the ferry terminal at Ludag, and two fine beaches.

Heading north you pass the modern church of Our Lady of Sorrows, built in 1963. At Cille Pheadair (Kilpheder) there are the remains of an ancient wheelhouse, excavated in 1952.

Hecla and Ben Mhor, South Uist

All along the main road tracks branch off to the west, leading down to lovely sandy beaches. At Aisgernis (Askernish) there is a nine hole golf course on sandy machair alongside the dunes and beach. On the east side of the main road is Minngearraidh (Mingarry) where the remains of a large chambered cairn can be found on the slope of Reineval.

At Milton there is a walled area with a cairn and a plaque to mark the birthplace of Flora MacDonald, famed for helping Bonnie Prince Charlie make his escape to Skye. There is an earth house and the remains of several store chambers at Na Doillaidh, all in a good state of preservation.

Leaving the main road a minor road makes a loop through the small townships of Bornais (Bornish), Ormacleit (Ormiclete) and Staoinebrig (Stoneybridge). It is at Ormacleit (Ormiclete) that you can see the remains of a castle built in 1701 for the Chief of Clanranald. It was burnt down only 14 years later.

At Tobha Mor (Howmore) there are a few examples of the once common tigh dubh (thatched or black house), which have now been classified as listed buildings. One has been converted into a Youth Hostel run by the Gatliff Trust. There is also the Church of Scotland with the traditional central communion pew.

Loch Druidibeg National Nature Reserve is one of the largest breeding grounds in the British Isles for the greylag goose. A permit can be obtained from the Scottish Natural Heritage warden at Groigearraidh (Grogarry) Lodge. There is a road from the lodge to Loch Sgioport (Skipport) which makes a very pleasant trip through remote country, bright with rhododendron bushes. The road ends with a steep hill down to a ruined pier.

Loch Skipport, South Uist

On the west slope of Rueval is the impressive 9 m granite statue of Our Lady of the Isles, erected in 1957. The view from the statue is well worth the short walk. Further up the hill is the Royal Artillery Range Control building, known locally as 'space city'. The firing area is located on the shore line south from Griminis (West Griminish), where the main supply and maintenance buildings are located. The range is used by visiting army and air force units to practise firing missiles at targets in a seaward direction. The Range Control Centre contains all essential safety features to ensure safe firing, such as surface and air radar, air traffic control, patrol launch control, computer and visual monitoring of all firings, as well as numerous other safety checks. Most of those working inside are denied the magnificent view just outside, extending from Skye in the east, the hills of Sutherland, the hills of Eilean Hearadh (Harris) and the Atlantic out to St Kilda, at the far end of the range.

A causeway has been built across the very large shallow Loch Bee, which at certain times of the year is populated with hundreds of mute swans.

Before reaching the causeway to Beinn Na Faoghla (Benbecula) there are roads off to the west, to the community of Iochdar (Eochar), and to the east to Loch Carnan, where there is a fuelling pier for the power station.

The new causeway to Beinn Na Faoghla (Benbecula) was opened in 1983 and stretches across the extensive cockle sands. The west side of the southern end is a very popular spot for collecting cockles, and at very low spring tides local people collect razor fish, and mussels on the north east shore.

EIRIOSGAIGH (ERISKAY)

Arrival and departure points

Car Ferry to/from Ludag, South Uist.
Passenger ferry to/from Ludag, South Uist and Eoligarry, Barra.

A small island about 1½ miles by 2½ miles lying between Uibhist A Deas (South Uist) and Eilean Bharraigh (Barra). The population of 200 are employed in fishing and crofting – a close knit community which takes a great pride in their island.

The sandy beach on the west side was the landing place of Bonnie Prince Charlie when coming to Scotland from France to gather the clans for the '45 rebellion.

The island also has traditional ponies which have been recognised as a rare breed and have been saved from extinction by the efforts of a preservation society. St Michael's Roman Catholic Church, built in 1903 and funded by the local fishing fleet, has a fine painting of the Baptism of Christ by John Duncan, RSW. The Angelus is rung three times a day on a ship's bell recovered from the German battleship *Derflinger*, sunk at Scapa Flow.

Between Eiriosgaigh (Eriskay) and Uibhist A Deas (South Uist) the wreck of the famous SS Politician may be seen at low tide. The 12,000 tonne ship was wrecked in 1941 carrying a general cargo, including 20,000 cases of whisky, which provided many throughout the islands with a supply of whisky for many years and a source of stories for even longer. A little pub on the island, opened in February 1988, has been named after the ship.

Eriskay

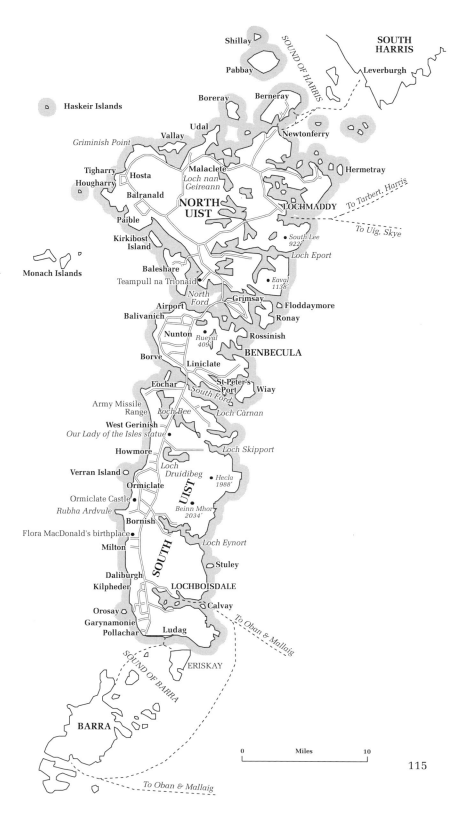

SOUTH HARRIS

Shillay
Pabbay
SOUND OF HARRIS
Leverburgh

Boreray
Berneray
Newtonferry

Haskeir Islands

Udal
Valley
Griminish Point
Malaclete
Loch nan Geireann
Hermetray

Tigharry
Hougharry
Hosta
Balranald
NORTH UIST
LOCHMADDY
To Tarbert, Harris

Paible
To Uig, Skye

Kirkibost Island
• *South Lee 922'*
Loch Eport

Baleshare
Teampull na Trìonaid •
• *Eaval 1138'*

Monach Islands

North Ford
Grimsay
Floddaymore

Airport
Balivanich
Ronay

Nunton
• *Rueval 409'*
Rossinish
BENBECULA

Borve
Liniclate

Eochar
St Peter's Port
Wiay
South Ford

Army Missile Range
Loch Bee
Loch Càrnan

West Gerinish
Our Lady of the Isles statue •
Loch Skipport

Howmore
Loch Druidibeg

Verran Island ○
• *Hecla 1988'*

Ormiclate
SOUTH UIST

Ormiclate Castle •
Rubha Ardvule
• *Beinn Mhor 2034'*

Bornish
Flora MacDonald's birthplace •
Loch Eynort

Milton
SOUTH

Daliburgh
Kilpheder
LOCHBOISDALE

Orosay ○
Calvay

Garynamonie
Pollachar
Ludag
To Oban & Mallaig

SOUND OF BARRA
ERISKAY

BARRA

| 0 | Miles | 10 |

115

To Oban & Mallaig

BEINN NA FAOGHLA (BENBECULA)

Arrival and departure points

Airport – British Airways to and from Stornoway, Eilean Bharraigh (Barra) and Glasgow.
Road – Linked to Uibhist A Tuath (North Uist) and Uibhist A Deas (South Uist), and consequently their ferry terminals.

The name Beinn Na Faoghla (Benbecula) means 'Mountain of the Fords', and recalls the time when a crossing could be made between the Uists over tidal sands. A road divides the island in two. The west side is low lying flat machair ground, where most of the island's farms and crofts are situated, as well as the lovely beaches. The east side has peaty moorland with numerous freshwater lochs and several large sea lochs overlooked by one hill, Rueval, rising to 149 m. Arriving by air the visitor might wonder that there is sufficient land between the lochs for an airport. The airport is in fact built parallel to a lovely sandy beach in the north west corner of the island and is surrounded by the modern buildings of the administration part of the Royal Artillery Range, Hebrides and RAF Benbecula. The range was first established in 1958, though most of the headquarters were built in 1971. There is also accommodation for 500 troops and families in the Baile A Mhanaich (Balivanich) area as well as integrated local authority housing. The mass of people plus the airport has made Baile A Mhanaich (Balivanich) the focal point of the island. Services, housing, shops, garages, health centre, school, fire services, postal sorting office, library and local authority offices are all situated here.

A mile north of the camp is Dun Gainmhich (Dunganachy), the site of an iron-age fort. It is possible to walk out to the dun, though there is only a trace of the walls left.

Baile A Mhanaich (Balivanich) was once the site of an old monastery, and just to the south is the ruin of Teampull Chaluim Chille, beside which is a well said to have healing properties. Further on is the lovely Culla Bay, behind which is Baile nan Cailleach (Nunton) where there are the ruined walls of a chapel and nunnery. There are several strange stories surrounding the nunnery at the time of the Reformation, but no documentation to give them substance.

The next bay heading south is Poll-na-Crann, more commonly known as 'stinky bay' due to the large deposits of seaweed washed up on the shore by the Atlantic swell. From the mid 18thC the seaweed was gathered to provide a source of income as well as to fer-

Tigh geal (white house) at Vallay Strand, North Uist

tilise the machair sands, but by 1820 the so called kelp boom was over. Seaweed is still gathered today for both alginate production and fertilising machair areas.

It was from Baile nan Cailleach (Nunton) in 1746 that Bonnie Prince Charlie left, dressed as Betty Burke, with Flora MacDonald to travel to Rossinish on the east coast, on their way 'over the sea to Skye'.

The ruins of Borve Castle are clearly visible from the road. This was probably built in the 14thC and was the stronghold of Clan Ranald of Beinn na Faoghla (Benbecula). The castle was burned down in the late 18thC century by clansmen who opposed their chief.

At Lionacleit (Linaclete) is the new sixth-year Community School, serving all three islands. The modern buildings contain a library, theatre, museum, championship size swimming pool, all weather sports track and hostel accommodation for school children. There is one small road off to the east coast and this can provide a pleasant outing. It leads to Peter's Port.

UIBHIST A TUATH (NORTH UIST)

Arrival and departure points

Loch Na Madadh (Lochmaddy) – Caledonian MacBrayne ferry to An Tairbeart on Eilean Na Hearadh (Tarbert, Harris) and Uig on Skye. *Triangular route, each leg about 2 hours.*
Port Nan Long (Newton Ferry) – *small passenger ferry* to An T-ob (Leverburgh) and car ferry to Eilean Bhearnaraigh (Berneray).

Loch Na Madadh (Lochmaddy) is the chief town and port of the island, with a population of about 300 and the location for the bank, post office, sheriff court, hotel, hospital and also the Tourist Information Centre and youth hostel. From the pier looking south are two large hills – North Lee & South Lee – rising to almost 304 m. Eagles can often be seen around this area. Just north of Loch Na Madadh (Lochmaddy) is Sponais (Sponish), with its own small harbour and once the main centre for processing seaweed.

Continuing north on the A865 there is a group of standing stones called Na Fir Bhreige (The False Men). Turning down towards Loch Portain (Lochportain) brings you to Dun Torcuill, an example of a Dun or fort located on a natural or artificial island in the middle of a loch, and usually known as a crannog. There is a path of stones from the shore to the island visible just under the surface. This type of fortified settlement is very common throughout the Western Isles and on many of the lochs you will see small islands with large piles of stones and sometimes even the outline of the walls. Dun Torcuill is one of the best preserved examples on the island and is worth a visit.

Further north on the road to Port Nan Long (Newton) is another crannog called Dun an Sticir, thought to be one of the last inhabited fortifications on the island and occupied as late as the 1600s. Driving up to the ferry terminal at Port Nan Long (Newton) provides lovely views of Hornish Strand, with a scattering of small islands. It is easy to spend many hours just watching the sea patterns changing with the tides as the swell comes in from the Atlantic. From Port Nan Long (Newton) the islands of Eilean Bhearnaraigh (Berneray), Pabbay and Boreray can be seen. Eilean Bhearnaraigh (Berneray) is the largest of these islands, about three miles long and one and a half miles wide with a population of about 150 surviving on crofting and fishing. A lovely green island with marvellous sandy beaches, the car ferry takes only a few minutes to cross from Port Nan Long (Newton), making the island well worth a visit.

Continuing on the main road past the beautiful sands of Bhalaigh (Vallay) Strand we come to Greinetobht (Grenitote) and Udal, where

Dr Alex MacLeod's tower at Scolpaig, North Uist

there is an archeological site recently excavated by Edinburgh University. For the more adventurous a walk to the end of the northern peninsula will be rewarded by the discovery of the mausoleum of the MacLeans of Boreray. Boreray is a now deserted island which can be seen off the point. Adjacent to the mausoleum is a small spring with associated rock carvings of a Christian cross and substantially more ancient cup and ring markings.

Just beyond Sollas there is a road to the left which leads to Ceann A Bhaigh (Bayhead), known as the committee road after the group who organised its construction during the famine relief schemes of the 19thC. There are similar roads on Eilean Na Hearadh and Eilean Leodhais (Harris and Lewis). Another example of famine relief work is the small tower standing on the remains of a dun in Loch Scolpaig. This is similar in style to the miniature castle at Uig on Skye. Scolpaig tower was built by Dr Alex MacLeod, chamberlain to the MacDonald estates, who was also responsible for the conspicuous latin cross half a mile south at Cille Pheadair (Kilpheder). This was erected in 1830 after being unearthed in a nearby burial ground.

The next settlement, Hosta, is a grass covered sand dune area where the North Uist games and cattle show are held annually in July and August. There is a lovely beach called Traigh Stir where the silver sand is washed by the breaking Atlantic swell. In the cliffs at Tigh A Ghearraidh (Tigharry) there is a natural rock arch and spouting cave commonly called the Kettle Spout. In the cave's roof at a distance of 9 m from the edge an opening has been worn through the

119

North and South Lee

upper portion of the rock giving a perpendicular shaft some 6 – 8 m across. During westerly storms the Atlantic rollers here break with enormous force, spouting water upwards through this vent to a height of more than 60 m. The Balranald Estate, once the seat of the MacDonald's of Griminis (Griminish), is now an RSPB Nature Reserve – during the summer there is a resident warden.

Eight miles off the coast are the Monach Isles (also known as Heisker). There is a disused lighthouse on Shillay, and none of the islands is now inhabited. Until the 16thC it was possible, it is said, at low tide, to walk to the islands, but that has now changed. Further south Baile Sear (Baleshare) used to be an island connected by a ford, but is now joined to Uibhist A Tuath (North Uist) by a causeway.

Clachan is at the junction of the main road to Loch Na Madadh (Lochmaddy). This road, apart from the junctions to Loch Eport and Langais (Langass), crosses the central peaty plain of Uibhist A Tuath (North Uist). On either side of the road the well cut lines of the peat banks can be clearly seen.

Just east of the Langais (Langass) road, on the slope of Ben Langais (Langass) is the chambered cairn of Bharpa Langais Relatively well preserved, it is 22 m long and 5.4 m wide, and is entered by means of a tunnel.

On the south side of Ben Langais is an oval shaped stone circle known as 'Pobull Thinn'. There is a pleasant drive along the twisting Loch Eport road to its end, and an interesting walk around the shores of Loch Obisang.

On the road south at Cairinis (Carinish) past the modern sheltered housing, are several historical sites. Teampull na Trionaid (Trinity Temple) was built about 1200 by Beatrice, daughter of Somerled of the Isles, perhaps on the foundations of an earlier ecclesiastical site. A further extension to the same building was made in the 16thC and is known as Teampull Clan A'Phiocair (Temple MacVicar).

The Battle of Cairinis (Carinish) in 1601 was the last battle between the MacLeods of Eilean Na Hearadh (Harris) and the MacDonalds of Uibhist (Uist). A ditch across the battlefield is known as Feithe Na Fala or ditch of blood, as it was so choked with dead bodies that the flowing water ran red.

The North Ford Causeway was built across several small islands to link Uibhist A Tuath (North Uist) to Griomasaidh (Grimsay) and then to Beinn Na Faoghla (Benbecula).

Griomasaidh (Grimsay) has a strong fishing community, specialising in shell fish – there are new storage tanks and harbour facilities at Kallin. A road encircles the island, making exploration easy.

Teampull na Trionaid

EILEAN NA HEARADH (HARRIS)

Arrival and departure points

An Tairbeart (Tarbert) – Caledonian MacBrayne ferry to Loch Na Madadh (Lochmaddy) on Uibhist A Tuath and Uig on Skye. *Triangular route, each leg about 2 hours.*
An T-ob (Leverburgh) – *small passenger ferry* to Eilean Bhearnaraigh (Berneray) and Port Nan Long (Newton Ferry) on Uibhist A Tuath (North Uist).

Ceann A Deas (South Harris)

A circular tour of some 45 miles can be made by travelling out on the west coast from An Tairbeart (Tarbert) and returning via the east coast. From the ferry terminal turn left on the main road sign posted to Roghadal (Rodel) on the A859. For the first few miles the road climbs up through some very rocky terrain giving some fine views over east Loch Tarbert, Eilean Scalpaigh (Scalpay) and on clear days Skye and the mainland. As the road starts to descend towards the sea notice the change in the landscape from the hard rocky terrain of the east coast to the sandy machair areas of the west as the Laxdale river flows out on to the beach at Losgaintir (Luskentyre). As we continue down the west coast there are many beautiful beaches – Losgaintir (Luskentyre), Horgabost, Nisabost, Na Buirgh (Borve), Sgarasta (Scarista) and An Taobh Tuath (Northton). You should always seek local advice before choosing a place to swim as some beaches are steeply shelving with strong currents and deep pools. All along this coast there are fine views across the Sound of Tarasaigh (Taransay) and northwards to the mountains of Ceann A Tuath Hearadh (North Harris). The island of Tarasaigh (Taransay) is named after St Taran and has several ancient sites and remains. Although well populated at the beginning of the century, there are now only two inhabitants.

Turning into the end of Horgabost village road you can see a group of large stones known as Coir Fhinn, believed to be the remains of a chambered cairn. Clach Micleoid is an interesting monolith on the western slope of Aird Nisabost worth a short walk for the vantage point at the top of the hill; there are several other standing stones in this area. Turn right into the village of An Taobh Tuath (Northton), past the genealogy centre run by Bill Lawson, and proceed to the machair at the foot of Chaipaval (365 m). This headland has several prehistoric sites and the ruined chapel of Rudh'an Teampuill. The chapel, thought to have been built about the same time as St Clements, measures about 6.4 x 3.4 m. Chaipaval provides a good, stiff walk with magnificent views in all directions. The steep cliffs at its far end provide nesting sites for a host of sea birds. On a clear day one has panoramic views of St Kilda out to the west, the hills of Uibhist A Tuath (North Uist), the Cuillins of Skye and the hills of Ceann A Tuath Na Hearadh (North Harris) to the north.

An T-ob (Leverburgh) was renamed (in English) after Lord Leverhulme, in 1923. It is a pretty little village with a shop, post office, tea room and craft centre at An Clachan. Remnants of Lord Leverhulme's attempt to turn Leverburgh into a large fishing port can be seen in the form of the foundations of large processing sheds near the pier which is also the departure point for the small passenger ferry to Uibhist A Tuath (North Uist).

Three miles from An T-ob is Roghadal (Rodel), dominated by the 12thC St Clements Church. The church is cruciform in plan and comprises nave, choir and two cross aisles and the dominant western Tower. There are three tombs inside the church of which the most notable, indeed one of the finest in Scotland, is built in the south wall of the choir. The tomb is arched and sculptured in remarkable detail and includes the MacLeod coat of arms, various saints and the apostles, whilst the Latin inscription is to the effect that the tomb was prepared by Alexander of Dunvegan. Below the church lies the Rodel Hotel which is in a lovely, quiet, position overlooking the small walled harbour and sheltered anchorage.

From Roghadal (Rodel) the circular route continues north through the striking moonscape scenery passing picturesque fishing villages. There is an interesting geological feature at Lingreabhagh (Lingerbay) – dazzling white anorthosite unique in size in the British Isles. Further on the villages of Fionnsbhagh (Finsbay), Manais (Manish), Geocrab and Leac A Li (Lackalea) lead to the youth hostel at Stocinis (Stockinish) and thence via Scadabhagh (Scadabay), Plocrabol (Plockrapool) and Drinisiadar (Drinishader) before joining the A859 just south of An Tairbeart (Tarbert). This east coast route, though narrow and winding, provides a stark contrast to the west side of the island. There are no large farms – instead very small areas cultivated as lazy beds gave a meagre living from the land. Many of the Eilean Hearadh (Harris) people survived on fishing.

An Tairbeart (Tarbert) is the main township of Eilean Na Hearadh (Harris), with a number of shops, a bank, post office, hotel, motel, restaurant, community centre and Tourist Information Centre. There is an interesting 10 mile return route along the Kyles Scalpay road through the villages of Urgha, Carragreich and Carnach. Just past Urgha on the north side of the road there are two hill tracks. One leads to the village of Marvig (Maaruig) on the shore of Loch Seaforth and linked to the A859, the other to the enchanting hamlet of Reinigeadal (Rhenigidale) where there is a Gatliff Trust Hostel. Keen climbers should refer to Norman Tennent's *The Islands of Scotland*

Lingerbay, South Harris

in the Scottish Mountaineering Club District Guide. The road ends at the village of Caolas Scalpaigh (Kyles Scalpay) overlooking Eilean Scalpaigh (Scalpay), which has a thriving fishing community. The car ferry service by Caledonian MacBrayne is operated every few hours and Eilean Scalpaigh (Scalpay) can provide an interesting and enjoyable afternoon walk. At the far eastern end of the island is Eilean Glas lighthouse, designed and built by the famous Stevenson brothers. Though still in use as a navigation mark the lighthouse buildings have been converted into holiday accommodation with a shop. Though there is no road to the lighthouse, the walk across the hills provides an excellent view across the Minch to Skye and the mainland.

Ceann A Tuath Na Hearadh (North Harris)

The most mountainous part of The Western Isles, its rugged and lonely splendour making it ideal for hill walking and climbing. This mountainous country is dominated by Cliseam (Clisham), the highest mountain in The Western Isles rising to over 792 m. Five miles north of An Tairbeart (Tarbert) on the A859 at Aird Asaig (Ardhasaig), the B887 road to Huisinis (Hushinish), though very narrow and winding, opens up some of the loveliest parts of Eilean Na Hearadh (Harris). Bun Abhainn Eadarra (Bunavoneadar) was until 1930 the centre of a thriving whaling industry and the foundations of

Amhuinnsuidhe Castle, North Harris

the slipways and the chimney of the whaling station are still to. be seen. Just before the village of Miabhag (Meavig) a walking track leads off north into the hills passing Loch Voshimid – where Sir J M Barrie found inspiration for his play *Mary Rose* – and connecting with a path which emerges onto the A859 near Aird A Mhulaidh (Ardvourlie). A second track at the village of Cliasmol leads into Loch Resort. Close to Amhuinnsuidhe Castle there is a hydro electric dam at Loch Cleostair, the power generated from here being almost sufficient to meet the needs of Eilean Na Hearadh (Harris). It was the first example of an arched dam to be constructed in The Western Isles. Passing through the castle gate at Amhuinnsuidhe brings you to a most picturesque sight – on your left there is a small river passing over the rocks on which salmon are seen to leap from pool to pool; then the road continues, passing the castle, built in 1868 by the Earl of Dunmore, and which is still a private residence. The road continues past the castle through the archway and a few miles further on there is the beautiful beach and machair at Huisinis (Hushinish) overlooking the island of Scarp.

Eilean Leodhais (Lewis)

Arrival and departure points

Stornoway to Ullapool, Caledonian MacBrayne *2 hours*.
Stornoway to Glasgow and Inverness,Stornoway to Beinn Na Faoghla
(Benbecula) and Eilean Bharraigh (Barra), British Airways.
Stornoway – Bus services to and from all parts of Eilean Leodhais
(Lewis) and Eilean Na Hearadh (Harris).

Visitors should remember that Sunday Observance is of great impor-
tance to the community and in addition to respecting this valuable
local custom, they should be prepared to plan their activities and
movements on the basis that neither public nor recreational facilities
nor shops, including petrol stations, are open on Sundays.

Stornoway (Pop 8,132) is the administrative and commercial capital of the Western Isles. It has a full range of medical services,
banks, shops, commercial services, hotels, guest-houses, restaurants,
YMCA, public and government offices as well as garages, car hire
firms and recreation facilities.

The Tourist Information Centre is situated in the town centre and
from this office a full range of books and pamphlets can be obtained
describing all places of interest in The Western Isles. Two publica-
tions are recommended for Stornoway. *Stornoway*, by Mary Bone,
describes a walk round the town, explaining monuments and historic
buildings. The other is *The Castle Grounds* by Peter Cunningham,
which is a description of the woods, their history and wildlife,
together with directions for the nature trails therein. The walks within these grounds provide magnificent views of the town and harbour,
and a variety of trees, shrubs and scenery found nowhere else in the
Western Isles.

Stornoway Harbour is one of the most sheltered natural harbours
in the west of Scotland, and though there has been a decline in the
fishing industry there is still considerable activity, with fishing and
small boats moving about the harbour. Once past the entrance,
Stornoway is fortunate in having a harbour that is only developed on
one side, leaving on the other a splendid view of purple rhododendrons, woods and grass lawn leading up to Lews Castle. There is a
fish market on Tuesday and Thursday evenings and it is well worth a
visit to see the variety of fish caught.

Moored in the harbour is *The Will*, Stornoway lifeboat station's
modern lifeboat. The Royal National Lifeboat Institution have been
present for more than 100 years in Stornoway and have one of the

EILEAN NA HEARADH (HARRIS)/EILEAN LEODHAIS (LEWIS)

The beautiful Traigh na Berie, Lewis

largest sea areas to cover. The fully manned Coastguard Rescue Co-ordinating Centre in Stornoway now also has the services of a full time rescue helicopter based at Stornoway Airport.

For the sporting there is an excellent 18 hole golf course open to visitors, who should apply to the clubhouse. Along Bayhead, approaching the centre, there is a bowling green, putting green and tennis court. At the Nicolson Sports Centre there is a swimming pool, badminton, squash, table tennis and a large gymnasium. There is a very active Sea Angling Club which welcomes visitors to its comfortable licensed clubhouse on South Beach quay. The club has its own boat and has been host to many national and international events. Trout and salmon fishing permits can be obtained from the Stornoway Trust Offices in the centre of Stornoway.

The town has a library with an extensive collection of local literature and staff that are very helpful in directing the visitor to any particular item of interest. In the Town Hall on South Beach Street there is a museum and gallery An Lanntair – which hosts a splendid collection of exhibitions and lectures throughout the year.

The road to the south from Stornoway is the A859 which leads to Tairbeart (Tarbert) and Ceann A Deas (South Harris). As it leaves Stornoway with the golf course and Lady Lever Park on the left hand side it passes, just on the boundary of the town, the dominant Lewis War Memorial erected to the fallen of the First World War but now containing, in addition, the roll of honour for the Second World War. There is a single track road which leads to Acha Mor (Achmore), dotted on either side with 'shielings', small cabins used by the people of the Point district when they used to spend the summer grazing their stock on the moor. Two miles further on there is a branch road leading to the large fabrication yard of Lewis Offshore at Arnish Point. This single track (dead end) road leads also to Arnish lighthouse (built in 1851 by Thomas Stevenson [1818-87], father of the famous Robert Louis Stevenson), and to Prince Charlie's Loch and Cairn, commemorating the fugitive Prince's hiding place at Kildun House (where the main fabrication shed now stands) in 1746 after the abortive '45 uprising.

The A859 continues over the moor to the junction at Liurbost (Leurbost) to the A858 which is the starting point for the Uig Route and the West Circle Route, described later. Passing through the villages of Lacasaidh (Laxay) and Baile-Ailein (Balallan) there are croft strips stretching out from the road on either side all the way along until the junction with the B8060 is reached. This road leads into the picturesque and unspoiled area of Pairc – the scene of a famous Deer Raid of 1887, when crofters, desperate for land, are alleged to have killed 200 deer to draw attention to their plight. Near Cromore on the south eastern shore of Eilean Chaluim Chille is the ruin of St Columba's Church, situated in a graveyard. Unfortunately this island can only be reached by ford at low tide. The road terminates at Leumrabhagh (Lemreway), although there is a circular branch round through the fishing villages of Marbhig (Marvig) and Calbost. Returning to the A858 the road continues over the moor via Airidh a Bhruaich and Ath Linne and Loch Seaforth into the hilly country of Ceann A Tuath Na Hearadh (North Harris).

Route to Uig

Having left Stornoway on the A859 as far as Liurbost (Leurbost) turn right onto the A858. At the village of Acha Mor (Achmore) half way along this road there is a fine view looking south west over Loch Trealaval and Loch Langavat to the hills of Ceann A Tuath Na Hearadh (North Harris), giving an indication of the size of the island. At Gearraidh Na H-Aibhne (Garynahine) take the left hand fork onto the B8011 and cross over Abhainn Dhubh, then a few miles later Abhainn Grimesta. These two rivers provide some of the best salmon fishing in The Western Isles, but the fishing rights belong to two large estates. Some four miles further on there is a right hand branch onto the B8059 leading to the island of Great Bernera, now joined to the mainland of Lewis by a road bridge over the Atlantic. Great Bernera is an interesting island with its small fishing villages, its cairns, standing stones and one or two duns or brochs.

The B8011 continues across the moor to the Pool of Cille Loch Roag, where the Morsgail River enters the sea loch. It is at this point that a track, past the recently rebuilt Morsgail Lodge, leads to the beehive dwellings on the north west side of Scalaval, and then on to

The Callanish Stones

the head of Loch Resort with subsequent moorland tracks through the hills by way of Glen Ulladale or Glen Stuladale to Amhuinn-suidhe and Miabhaig (Miavaig) respectively. These walks are long and arduous and should not be undertaken without suitable gear and local advice. Continuing on the B8011 the road leads to the small village of Giosla (Gisla) with its power station and abundance of conifers and rhododendrons, and then on to Glen Bhaltos (Valtos). This gorge was a glacial meltwater channel and is the only one of its kind in Lewis. The road to the left leads to Timsgearraidh (Timsgarry) and the Uig sands at the village of Eadar Dha Fhadhail (Ardroil), where there are miles of sand dunes and machair. On the south side of the bay close to the base of a small hill known as Eornal are the scattered remains of at least two small hut circles. Several pottery fragments and various utensils were found here, and in 1831 the now famous walrus ivory 'Lewis Chessmen' were found buried in the sand. There were 78 pieces belonging to at least eight incomplete chess sets. Some are in the National Museum of Antiquities in Edinburgh but most are in the British Museum in London, along with 14 ivory draught board pieces and a belt buckle, which have been estimated to have been used around the 11-12thC.

The road carries on for a few miles past a sand and gravel quarry on the site of an 'esker' or glacial sand deposit, now containing fish hatching tanks, to Breanais (Brenish), with tracks to Mealasta (Mealista) along which there are superb views from the precipitous cliffs.

At Glen Bhaltos (Valtos) the road to the right leads to Miabhaig (Miavaig), where, if you keep left, you will come to the picturesque beach at Cliff, which is not safe for swimming. Half way up the hill is

The whalebone arch at Bragar

an outdoor activity centre run by the Western Isles Council. Past the village of Bhaltos (Valtos) and Cnip (Kneep) is the beautiful Traigh na Berie, a mile of safe sandy beach with a large flat machair area very popular for caravans and camping. The machair is a duck sanctuary and at the far end of the beach the marshy area is fed by a small stream from a loch. On this stream are the remains of four horizontal water-wheel type grain mills (traditionally a Norse design) which are thought to have been in use up to 150 years ago.

West Side Route

Circular from Stornoway and return via Barabhas (Barvas). The journey to Gearraidh Na H-Aibhne (Garynahine) takes the traveller to the starting point of the West Side circular tour, which for the short stay visitor is perhaps the most comprehensive and rewarding in all aspects of rural life and culture on Eilean Leodhais (Lewis). From Gearraidh Na H-Aibhne (Garynahine) the A858 leads to the famous Calanais (Callanish) Stones, the equal of Stonehenge in historical value. The site is about 33 m above sea level on a promontory extending into Loch Roag, from which there is a commanding view of the surrounding area. The stones, erected about 4000 years ago, are in the form of a Celtic cross, with a chambered cairn in the centre. The full significance of these stones is not yet known, though there certainly seem to be astronomical connections, especially with the rising and setting of the moon. The central cairn was used as a burial centre for many centuries after construction (see the *Standing Stones* by G Ponting). There is also a craft centre and tea room as well as a

Clach an Truiseil

number of satellite megalithic circles.

At Breascleit (Breasclete) the former shore station of the Flannan Isles lighthouse, famous for the mysterious disappearance of the three keepers in December 1900, immortalised in verse by Wilfred Gibson, has now been converted into flats. The pier at Breascleit (Breasclete) has been improved with the addition of a fish drying factory constructed by the Highlands and Islands Development Board, but this unfortunately proved to be rather a disappointment and is now used for the manufacture of medical preparations from fish oil. Three miles further on a detour into the picturesque little village of Tolastadh a Chaolais (Tolasta Chaolais) is worthwhile. Re-emerging on to the A858 leads within a couple of miles to the Carlabhagh (Carloway) Broch - the best preserved structure of its type in The Western Isles. The broch is worth the steep climb up the hill, as this drystone habitation has survived for almost 2000 years. The remaining outer wall is 9 m high and slopes inwards, with an inner wall which rises vertically, leaving chambers between the walls. There are stairs to galleries at various heights, constructed of large slabs of stone. The view from the broch is quite splendid and summarises the island way of life; the harsh rocky hills, the lovely lochs, the peat banks, the old croft buildings with their small cultivated area of lazy beds and the modern fish farming cages.

Passing through the village of Carlabhagh (Carloway), Lord Leverhulme's proposed fishing port on the west coast of Lewis, a small branch road leads to the deserted 'black house' village at Gearrannan (Garenin). These houses have now been preserved and provide hostel accommodation by the Gatliff Trust. This example of a 19thC settlement is well worth visiting to catch the atmosphere and enjoy a splendid view over the rolling Atlantic.

At Dail Mor (Dalmore) and Dail Beag (Dalbeg) there are two fine secluded beaches where you may enjoy a picnic or an evening sunset. The next main village on the A858 is the sprawling township of Siabost (Shawbost) with its old Norse mill at the south end (500 m into the moor from the road) and its interesting - but as yet unclassified and professionally exhibited - treasure trove of Hebridean artefacts at the museum. Further north in the village of Bragar is an archway formed from the jawbone of a blue whale, and some 2 miles past this the road branches to the Black House Museum at Arnol. This well cared for monument is certainly worth a visit. Inside are traditional furniture and utensils, as well as a peat fire to give the true atmosphere. Finally at Barabhas (Barvas) the A857 road cuts back across the moor to Stornoway, or alternatively northwards to the Butt of Lewis.

Route to Nis (Ness)

This journey, like the West Side Circular Route, makes an interesting day trip from Stornoway, returning in the late afternoon or early evening. Shortly after Barabhas (Barvas) the first turning on the left into Baile an Truiseil (Ballantrushal) village takes the visitor to Clach an Truiseil, a magnificent monolith, some 5.7 m high, which by local tradition is the spot of the last big battle in Lewis between the Morrisons of Nis (Ness) and the MacAulays of Uig. Further along the A857 in the village of Siadar (Shader) the first road to the left leads to the ruins of Teampull Pheadair, now a grass covered rectangular mound, almost 10.6 m long, and dating from the late Iron Age period. In the middle of the village a rough track leads to the circle and standing stones of Clach Stein, a fragmented tomb with ten vertical slabs surrounding the burial chamber. Neither of the places is clearly signposted, but walkers or zealous historians will find the effort of seeking them out worthwhile.

The main road continues through typical crofting villages, Coig Peighinnean (Fivepenny Borve), Gabhsunn (Galson), Dail (Dell), Swainabost (Swainbost), Tabost (Habost) to Lional (Lionel) and Port Nis (Port of Ness). This small harbour is now unfortunately silted up and only used by small boats, though it is pleasant to walk around and watch the gannets diving from a great height into the sea.

Each September the *guga* hunters land their catch of young gannets geese or *gugas*, which they have caught on the island of Sula Sgeir, 30 miles north of Eilean Leodhais (Lewis). The *gugas* are considered such a delicacy by the people of Lewis that they are in great demand, and should be ordered in advance if you wish to try one (see Hebridean Dishes, page 75).

The Rubha Robhanais (Butt of Lewis) lighthouse marks the northernmost extremity of the Western Isles, with magnificent views over the Atlantic and across to the Sutherland hills on the mainland. Looking south the grass slopes are lined for miles with rows of lazy beds, and beyond that the miles of fencing which divide the land into small crofts.

At Eoropaidh (Eoropie) is the ancient Teampull Mholuaidh (St Moluag's Church), probably built around the 12thC, with side chambers added at a later date. The church was restored to its present condition in 1912 and services are now conducted on certain Sundays by the priest of St Peter's Episcopal Church, Stornoway.

Finally there are two short excursions from Stornoway. The first, on the B895 along the north west side of Broad Bay, passes through the villages of Tunga (Tong), Col (Coll), Griais (Gress) and Tolastadh (North Tolsta) to the two magnificent beaches of Traigh Mhor and Garry. There is a popular caravan and camping site at Col (Coll).

The second short route, by the A866, leads east from Stornoway skirting the south eastern edge of Broad Bay and passing Stornoway Airport, taking the visitor to the church of St Columba at Ui. This is well worth a visit, as it has the tombs of the last Chiefs of the Macleods of Lewis, as well as one of the Seaforths. W C Mackenzie in his *History of the Outer Hebrides* states 'the Lewis priory, dedicated to St Catan at, or near Stornoway' and was 'Attached to the church of St Columba at Ui'. Presumably he uses the word attached not in a literal but in a figurative sense. At the end of the A866 is Tiumpan Head lighthouse, which affords fine views of the mainland hills. A right hand diversion into Paibil (Bayble) leads to a sheltered little harbour where one can picnic and relax. The Eye Peninsula is now very much a suburb of the Stornoway conurbation, yet it has retained much of its crofting and fishing background.

The Butt of Lewis

134

Suggested Further Reading

Atkinson, Robert. *Island Going.* Collins.

Baxter, Colin and Crumley, Jim. *St Kilda.* Colin Baxter Photography.

Burnett, Ray. *Benbecula.* The Mingulay Press.

Cameron, A.D. *Go Listen to the Crofters.* Acair.

Cooper, Derek. *The Road to Mingulay.* Routledge & Keegan Paul.

Cooper, Derek. *Hebridean Connection.* Routledge & Keegan Paul.

Cunningham, Peter. *Birds of the Outer Hebrides.* Melven Press.

Cunningham, Peter. *A Hebridean Naturalist.* Acair.

Darling, F. Fraser and Boyd, J. Morton. *The Highlands and Islands.* Collins.

Geddes, A. *The Isle of Lewis and Harris.* (Edinburgh, 1955).

Grant, James Shaw. *Discovering Lewis and Harris.* John Donald.

Grant, James Shaw. *Highland Villages.* Hale.

Grant, James Shaw. *Stornoway & The Lews.* Thin.

Grant, James Shaw. *Surprise Island.* Thin.

Grant, James Shaw. *Their Children Will See.* Hale.

Grant, James Shaw. *The Gaelic Vikings.* Thin.

Grant, James Shaw. *The Hub of my Universe.* Thin.

Hunter, James. *The Making of the Crofting Community.* John Donald.

Johnson, Alison. *A House by the Shore.* Gollancz.

MacAulay, Rev. Murdo. *Aspects of the Religious History of Lewis.*

MacDonald, A.M. *A Lewis Album.* Acair.

MacDonald, Donald. *Lewis.* Gordon Wright Publishing.

MacDonald, Donald. *Tales and Traditions of the Lews.* (Stornoway, 1967).

MacDonald, Finlay J. *Crowdie and Cream.*

MacDonald, Finlay J. *Crottal and White.*

MacDonald, Finlay J. *The Corncrake and the Lysander.*

MacGregor, Helen and Cooper, John. *Barra.* Canongate Publishing, Edinburgh.

MacKenzie, W.C. *Colonel Colin MacKenzie.* (Edinburgh, 1952).

MacKenzie, W.C. *History of the Outer Hebrides.* (Paisley, 1903).

MacKenzie, W.C. *Short History of the Highlands of Scotland.* (Paisley, 1907).

MacKenzie, W.C. *The Book of the Lews.* (Paisley, 1919).

MacKenzie, W.C. *The Highlands and Islands of Scotland.* (Edinburgh, 1937, revised 1949).

MacKenzie, W.C. *The Western Isles.* (Paisley, 1932).

Macleod, Charles. *Devil in the Wind.* Gordon Wright.

Martin, Martin. *A Description of the Western Isles of Scotland.* (London, 1716; Glasgow, 1884).

Morton Boyd, J. *The Hebrides – a Natural History.* (HarperCollins).

Murray, W.H. *The Islands of Western Scotland.* Eyre Methuen.

Nicholson, N. *Lord of the Isles.* (London, 1955).

Perrott, David. *The Western Islands Handbook.* Kittiwake Press.

Simpson, W.D. *Portrait of Skye and the Outer Hebrides.* (1967).

Swire, O. *The Outer Hebrides and their Legends.* (Edinburgh, 1966).

Stephen, Ian and Maynard, Sam. *Malin, Hebrides, Minches.* Dangaroo Press.

Stephen, Ian. *Living at the Edge.* Aberdeen Peoples Press.

Stephen, Ian. *As an Fhearran.* Mainstream Publishing.

Tennent, Norman. *The Islands of Scotland.* Scottish Mountaineering Club District Guide.

Thompson, Francis. *The Crofting Years.* Luath Press.

Thompson, Francis. Harris Tweed. *The Story of an Island Industry.* David and Charles.

Thompson, Francis. *The National Mod.* Acair.

Thompson, Francis. *St. Kilda and other Hebridean Outliers.* David and Charles.

Thompson, Francis. *The Western Isles.* Batsford.

Wilkie, Jim. *Metagama.* Mainstream Publishing.

The Island Blackhouse. HMSO.

Tong. The Story of a Lewis Village. Stornoway Gazette.

INDEX